10

ARTIST
COMMANDMENTS

10

ARTIST
COMMANDMENTS

10 **Principles** to Create Enduring Success
in the Business of Entertainment.

J.R. MCKEE

ISBN: 979-8-9885151-0-4 – Paperback
eISBN: 979-8-9885151-1-1 – ePub

Library of Congress Control Number: 2023916691

Printed in the United States of America   0 9 1 2 2 3

⊗This paper meets the requirements of ANSI/NISO Z39.48-1992 (Permanence of Paper)

CONTENTS

INTRODUCTION

After eighteen years in the music business, I've come to realize that there are ten principles that every creative person who wants to succeed must live by. And that is what *10 Artist Commandments* promises to give you for a successful, long-lasting career in the arts: ten principles to live by. Within these pages lies a lucrative career that many never thought was possible to achieve.

The difference between this book and the hundreds of others that are out there is that I have made my success as an entrepreneur in the music industry. However, I don't credit my success to my creative talent. I credit it to the fact that I am able to do what I do because I have an entrepreneurial spirit which is a very different energy than "I can sing so make me a star."

Having an entrepreneurial approach to your art puts you, as an artist, in the driver's seat of your career. This is why you will see things in this book that may surprise you. Please take it from me that being in charge of your own destiny, especially in the entertainment world, will give you longevity that you may have never thought possible.

In my experience, the creative's career life cycle often looks like this: A creative artist starts from the bottom, shoots to the top (if they are extremely talented and lucky), and then they inevitably fall off. The "next-level" artist's trajectory is that they start from the bottom, rise to the top, and then create new levels. (Off the top of my head, Rihanna's name comes to mind.)

The other thing that I have observed about artists who have been able to sustain enduring success is their incredible ability to build a substantial audience and engage with them in a way that makes their fans deeply loyal and invested in whatever they do. These next-level artists have created engagement so thoroughly that they have amassed a fan base that has unconditional love for them and their art. This frees the artist to grow, change, and evolve without much pushback from their fans since the fans feel as though they have been part of their journey all along-sort of a "ride or die." When fans feel like they know the artist personally, they genuinely understand when and why they have the need to grow and change.

10 Artist Commandments is guaranteed to secure longevity and intentional elevation when appropriately executed by any creative, no matter who you are. These 10 Commandments are timeless because they aren't necessarily about technology, social media, or media, period. These Commandments are about the artists, the art, and the relationship between the artists and the fans. And, of course, the business of art.

It is my intention that these 10 Commandments are not focused on the art itself, but are focused on helping artists understand the financial and societal value of their art. I want to encourage artists to look at the multiple aspects of a career in the arts and the inherent relationship between an artist and their fan base. Lastly, this book will show you the importance of knowing how to adapt your art for longevity. Most importantly, *10 Artists Commandments* is about achieving the highest level of success using your God-given talent. All of these principles are ubiquitous to art, artists, and fans.

The biggest changes in the art world have been and will continue to be 1) technology, 2) ever-changing social attitudes, and 3) new outlets and platforms. The good news about technology is that it has irreversibly changed the way that art is produced. Never before have artists had the autonomy to create their art when and how they wish, reach their fan base directly, and monetize their art in many different ways to ensure the possibility of multiple streams of income as well as the ability to venture into new art forms based on their original talent.

We have all seen rappers turn into actors and singers turn into TV talk show hosts, and we have even seen rappers turn into politicians. It's all possible once you let your presence be known. This book will offer new perspectives on what it truly means to be an artist. Hopefully, you have mastered your art, but there is so much more to it.

I decided to write this book as a music executive who has too often watched artists lose opportunities because they were unprepared for the rigors of a successful career. When I say unprepared, I don't mean a lack of talent or even a lack of work ethic. I mean the lack of knowledge required to have a long-term career. There are plenty of technicalities, audience hacks, adaptation, and lots more that come with an entertainment career, not just a great voice, great writing skills, or a wonderful eye for fashion. When I say technicalities, I am referring to intricate knowledge of your craft. For example, understanding the full scope of valuation of your art. You must understand the implications and nuances of the business that you are in and familiarize yourself with legal terms, contracts, laws and boundaries of intellectual property, perpetuity, percentages owned and earned, royalties, streaming royalties, advances, etc. Another thing to think about, which can also be considered a technicality, is really knowing what your chosen art entails. Just because you can write lyrics that are catchy or are an example of masterful wordplay, even being a songwriter has some technicalities, too, says Blu June, Grammy award-winning songwriter for Rihanna and Beyoncé. "To be a successful songwriter, you must understand melody and how to use your voice as an instrument. That is what sets apart a good song vs. a great song."

When I mention audience hacks, I am referring to knowing how to build loyalty by employing social media programs that can give access to your fans to let them into your world. By doing this, you will create a feeling of specialness for your fans that goes a long way in a competitive and crowded sea of artists. I have seen this effort pay off in dividends. Today's fans don't want to just know you through sound bites from interviews and talk show appearances. They want to know what you do when you are not creating music. They want to know what inspires you; they want to know what makes you angry. Fans want to know your spouse's name and the names of your children. They want to know your *heart*. Lastly, the word adaptation is the ability to learn new ways to keep your audience engaged with you and your music. As an artist, it is inevitable that your art will eventually have to adapt to new trends, sounds, and collaborations that will give your music wings. That is if you are planning for a long career. Just think of Elton John collaborating with Britney Spears and Dua Lipa, causing his old songs to become new again.

I had all types of artists in mind when writing this book, not just recording artists but writers, visual artists, actors, producers, etc. You may have been writing music, performing, or acting for years already. There is a reason that you are reading this book. This book is intended to take your creative career to next-level status. It will take you time, and the courage to just be yourself. I am also aware that everyone who is investing in their artistic dreams cannot always immediately attain management or afford a video budget or even an expensive lawyer. However, I assure you if you trust me by understanding and implementing the foundational principles in these 10 Commandments, making your dreams come true will be significantly more attainable.

As you read these chapters, I ask that you become more

comfortable within your own artistic skin. By doing that, you will be prepared to climb the ladder to success. I beg of you to be at peace knowing everyone's timeline is unique. Therefore, *do not rush your craft.* Instead, create a community of supporters who will feel connected to you because they see you living in your truth and being authentic. With that simple approach, you will attract the perfect audience and opportunities for your talents when you have the insight to dissect your life experiences (good and bad) and share them with honesty and vulnerability. There is no one's experience that is unique; however, the way that you cope and overcome is where your individuality means everything. Your story, no matter what it is, will resonate with millions of people if you take advantage of this amazing opportunity to create a platform that your precious talent has created for you. *Do it justice.*

J.R. McKee

COMMANDMENT

1

TELL THE TRUTH

"The truth shall set you free."

John 8:32

*Did you hear about the rose that
grew from a crack in the concrete?
Proving nature's laws wrong, it
learned to walk without having feet.
Funny it seems, but by
keeping its dreams,
it learned to breathe fresh air.
Long live the rose that
grew from concrete
when no one else ever cared.*

Tupac Shakur

Are you a rose who grew from concrete? I like this metaphor because it points to the uniqueness and beauty of every artist, no matter where they come from. It also highlights the fact that the rose is notable *because* it came from concrete. No matter how large and successful you dream of being, the fact remains that you will never be able to set yourself apart from the truth of whence you came. If you are not authentic about what you grew from or where you've been, you are already stunting your own growth. The biggest mistake you can make in your career is starting at the finish line instead of beginning where you are: the concrete. Pretending you're somewhere further than you are (at this point) takes the fun out of your growth on the unique journey forward. Ironically, when it comes to hip-hop artists, there is the opposite problem. I have seen artists that are not from "the hood" but pretend they are with added details of street life that are comedic and take away from the authenticity of their music.

I am sure you have heard the adage, "Birds of a feather stick together." Disingenuous people are drawn to others like them. And that is *not* whom you want to attract. People that are fake are only drawn to the surface and, therefore, will never be genuine followers of yours. That kind of person is often fickle and bad for artists because they will move on to the next new artist who comes out with a hit record before you know it. Fake people do not have the capacity to be loyal.

Artists who "fake it 'til they make it" usually don't take the time to consider what will happen when their money runs out, and they still haven't truly made it. Those artists who have experienced this usually give up or have to go back to square one, maybe even becoming worse off than they were before.

As an artist, I know that your heart and spirit are authentic, which means you are already *vulnerable*. An artist's vulnerability comes from our unique ability to feel all of our emotions. We are able to love and admire beauty; we are able to feel the depths of heartbreak and loss. This is why we are able to write so beautifully, paint so accurately, or sing like an angel. It is your soul speaking when you are doing your art. And, sharing your gift is a gift for you and your fans. It is an honorable pursuit and puts us in the most vulnerable positions imaginable.

All of this beauty and discomfort is what makes art so important to the world. It is the only place where truth can be found. Choosing to be authentic even when you have no team, no clout, no fame, no streams, no sales, no income, and no platform is always your best bet.

Vulnerability Sells

I've worked with numerous artists over two decades, and the common thread is artists (no matter how amazing their work is) are human. Everyone has fears, insecurities, anxieties, and painful memories. So as a creator, you must constantly tap into your humanity to connect with your fans.

By now, I hope you recognize that your connection to your fans is everything, and the number one way to create a connection is by sharing what makes you human. Our vulnerability is one of our greatest assets because it is the way that true connection is possible. No one wants to believe that you are perfect; they want to see parts of themselves in you, even the weakest parts. Once a fan sees themself in you, you give them the hope that they can overcome their obstacles like you did. And if you haven't overcome yours yet, you will create supporters that will do anything to see you succeed. By rooting for you, they are rooting for themselves. But first, you have to allow yourself to be vulnerable enough to share the things in your life that are hard to share, often dreadful, painful, violent, egregious, or tragic. Those things that may cause you shame are what fuel your art. Without even knowing your story, trust me, there are worse. Humanity is messy. The complexities of being human always include love, lust, sex, divorce, violence, substance abuse, mental health issues, poverty, and wealth. Without those elements of humanity, there would be no art. Remember that. By telling your story, you are always in the right place.

Simply put, no matter where you are in life or what you have done, or what has been done to you, it is a mistake to portray yourself any other way than the truth. Whether you are rich or poor, there is no escape from the issues and stress factors of life. And what I've discovered, if I'm being honest, is that neither money nor poverty will ever be the true cause of our discontent.

Before sharing your truth, you must embrace it. An example:

I was silent, watching,
scoping the scene
Cool kid, if you know what I mean
But the world I was in
Full of currency and sin
Pops worked his ass off
He did everything he can
Man, he prolly made a mill
But he never had a plan
So we was looking fly, but
we finally had to land
I thought that I was better cuz I never
popped a zan Shit, I got addictions
too but would judge another man
I could barely keep my dick in my
muthafucking pants
That itself runs deep
I can barely fucking sleep
She was creeping in my sheets
And I never said a peep
Never had the will to speak
I was muthafucking weak

Man, I knew that shit was wrong
thought about it all week
Then I thought it was the norm even
tho we had to sneak
Then I met the homie Ralph
He was doing the same shit
Man, this shit was really sick
We was only fucking six
Know It fucked my head up

LaRussell, from "Dollar 2 The Rich"

These are lyrics from the song "Dollar 2 the Rich" by artist/entrepreneur LaRussell. Hailing from the Bay area, his lyrics are a perfect example of an artist who is known for sharing his story authentically and unapologetically. Although the experiences that this song depicts are real, there is a lot more to this artist than just a rough childhood story. But he wants people to know his story so that his fans understand that he has overcome so much of his past by making music, but also by making a difference. LaRussell refuses to tell his story in interviews. He says, "It's all in the music. These things are too deep to sum up. My story is just really sharing my experience—everything is easy to share through music." When speaking about his creative process, he says, "With the songs, I don't just 'write it.' It is the way that I process it for myself. The intention of the song is to release it. The world benefits from therapy, but art is free. Every person who has depression or happy moments, the art just helps you get through it. It is a necessity in society."

I always encourage artists to understand their

experiences and look at them from all angles. Most times, we don't understand why we are the way we are until we go back and unravel what has happened to us. How can you be honest if you haven't looked deep into the chaos disturbing your inner peace? You cannot share your truth if you are not living in it.

Have you ever noticed that those who are unapologetically comfortable with themselves are usually the most well-received? Think about Cardi B, Chuck D, Lizzo, Lil Nas X, James Baldwin, Jean-Michel Basquiat, and Dave Chappelle. All of these artists have or will go down in history for their extremely bold, eccentric personalities. These are also artists who have experienced their share of "hate" from the masses, but the hatred has paled in comparison to the undying love their fans have for them. These artists have been criticized for being conceited, cocky, radical, dangerous, and even un-American. Although they may have been reviled in the news media or in social media, they are names that you will never forget. Their careers skyrocketed just because they were being their authentic selves.

People who don't like or prefer their style of music, art, or comedy were simply not meant to be their fans. However, for those for whom their art resonates, they will be the ride-or-die type of fan that every artist needs. These artists will forever be praised and uplifted for their courage to be who they are with no apology. They are inspirations for being oneself, and people never forget the person who allowed them to be free.

So, to artists, I say, just do *you*. Don't ever be afraid to stand by your art, your true story, or your beliefs. They are what make you unique and someone who will always pique the interests of others. As an experiment, just try showing parts of yourself that you may not even have shared with people who love you. You will be surprised by how much love people will show you when you start owning yourself and your real-life experiences. You will never be the only one who has experienced it. And they will be forever in your debt for showing them what being free looks like.

People who are not ashamed to tell their truths are able to consistently produce more authentic and impactful content, even without a big record deal, famous gallery shows, or large film studios behind them.

> *As artists, you have the power to say whatever you want, but the believability factor is what will endear your fans to you.*
>
> J.R. McKee

THE ART OF THE MESSAGE

An artist's authenticity is what makes art of all kinds so addictive. Music, acting, visual arts, dance, film, writing, and photography all have the power to create a massive platform for an artist to share their message. An artist's message must be one of authenticity, accuracy, and truth. Although your fans will spend most of their time watching you online, on TV, or on the movie screen, your authenticity will show in your eyes, your body language, and the emotion in your voice.

That is what makes some artists' career soar, racking up more followers than others. Think about it like this, every time someone "follows" you, they are in solidarity with you. And that solidarity with many adds up to a flourishing group of loyal fans. The truth in your message is your superpower, instantly connecting you with people with whom you resonate.

As an artist, your message is your most potent weapon; use it as ammunition. For a writer or lyricist, your message is in your words; as an actor, your message is in the roles that you choose to play; as a visual artist, your message is in the subject matter of your art. Is it political, Afrocentric, historical, or abstract? The bottom line is what you are saying to people represents you and your beliefs. Your art is an extension of you.

So, before you aim your weapon, consider the target you intend to hit. It is a major mistake to craft words together for the sake of your lyrics sounding *cool.* Once you make this mistake, you will eventually lose your ability to connect, no matter how much masterful wordplay is displayed. The message is what captures people; it is what makes them think on a deeper level. Artists, before you step up to the microphone, ask yourself, Which message do I intend to send out into the world? Whom am I looking for? With whom will my words resonate? What have I been through that I can share and make a difference in someone's life? In sharing your truth, not only can you help heal a listener, you can heal yourself by speaking your truth aloud. Sharing your mistakes helps others avoid the same downfalls. This can also be true when sharing perspectives about things you've thought about or witnessed and may have a unique insight on.

When Tupac recorded "Brenda's Got a Baby," his purpose was more than rapping about a young girl who got pregnant; he hoped to stop other young girls from making the same mistake as Brenda. If you intend to create a true fan base, send notable messages that heal people and show them a way to better themselves. When we look at the work of painter Ernie Barnes, and his famous painting *Sugar Shack*, his work immediately showcases the beauty of Black bodies. His work is known for elucidating African American life. The same goes for Alice Walker and Toni Morrison, two legendary authors who tell holistic stories of Black life in order for African Americans to see themselves and have a better understanding of their experiences and pain.

We also see messaging in different contexts, such as in film. Think about Tyler Perry's Madea movies. Those movies are very specifically geared toward the African American audience to whom Tyler Perry wants to communicate. Despite the comedic context in which he creates laughable characters, there is always a space for a message that is very targeted for his audience. Because he chooses these specific themes: religion, respect, marriage, etc., as the creator, he is actually showing his authenticity and the pain surrounding the Black community. Cleverly, he has couched these powerful messages in the creation of outrageously comedic characters that soften the blow of the truth-telling he is actively doing.

JEALOUSY AND ENVY

Although all art is sacred, some art resonates more than others, and that is because of conditions that are often out of the artists' hands. So don't immediately blame yourself or your art for low sales or not being "famous" yet. The reasons for your lack of immediate success could be a lack of effective management, timing, a shift in cultural attitudes, the political climate, etc. Success is a crossing of preparation meeting opportunity, and those two roads just may not have crossed for you yet.

If you have a truly entrepreneurial spirit, when your art has been released and is not selling as well as you'd like, you must problem-solve and make new choices. However, the most important thing you can do is: Do not become a jealous artist. Jealousy is a waste of energy. You can never have what someone else has. You have to get what is meant for you.

One of the downfalls for new artists is that they allow jealousy to get the best of them, and they lose focus on creating unforgettable art. I have seen artists who actually feel entitled to the lifestyles they see others enjoying while they have no idea what that artist has gone through to get where they are. You may think you have some idea because of what you heard or read on social media, but let me tell you, as an industry insider, it is a small percentage of what they have actually had to suffer to be who they are. And, for those young artists who tend to hate on artists whom they feel have "sold out," that is the absolutely wrong way to think about it. We will look at this later when we get to the last commandment: Adapt or Die.

> *I am older now and have tapped into the things that matter. Society has us thinking that outside is where it is, but I think when we focus inward, we have the most light.*
>
> Eric Bellinger

WHO DO YOU THINK YOU ARE?

Every person can choose who they want to be. And while it is true that our circumstances, surroundings, and exposures make up who we are, these are just the beginnings of anyone's story. For each of us, there will be a significant difference between who you are today and who you will be in the future. If you feel *not-so-great* about who you are today, you can decide to do the things necessary to create the life you want. To do this, change old habits that no longer serve you in order to upgrade your circumstances and surroundings. Despite what you have been told about who you are and who people would like you to be, only you can decide who you are and will become.

As we grow, our exposures and experiences force us to

become our own person, separate from our parents, siblings, and even our friends. This process is called individuation, becoming an individual apart from your family. We have seen many examples of two siblings who were raised by the same parents in the same house, and one child becomes a superstar and, sadly, the other an addict. In another household, we've seen one sibling become a successful parent and the other sibling have no desire to care for their children. It is profound to see that no two people share the same truth, despite the DNA. Everyone's reactions and recollections of trauma and experiences differ. For instance, a household could have a father who is stern about saving money, but one child may grow to become great with money, saving, investing, and spending responsibly, whereas the second child may grow to spend irresponsibly, believing their father was a cheapskate. The same thing goes for households with workaholic parents. One child may grow up thinking you have to overwork in order to make money to be happy, while their sibling may argue that having money isn't everything and find that quality time with family is more important. The reality is what truly defines you is your mindset, which is your unique vision of the world.

I give these examples to encourage you to think about where you fit into the world. How did your upbringing influence your mindset? Make no mistake, your parents, friends, television, films, and social media have fed your mind your entire life and played a big part in how you think about yourself and others. Once you decide who you are based on your history, it will then be time to decide who you want to be. What you feed your mind from this day forward will determine your success in the journey to become who you have chosen to be. It is not enough to say who you want to be; you must go into action to define your true self. Wherever you are today, begin feeding your body, mind, and soul with only healthy things that inspire you to become your best self.

Finding yourself is the most challenging thing you can do. And the most worth it. Often, people have no idea who they are outside of the opinions of others. As a burgeoning artist, I suggest that you spend time alone to learn your greatest attributes and practice mastering whatever brings out the best artist in you because your talent and truth will attract *your* community.

As an artist, it is okay to take a break from your art to develop yourself. Perhaps instead of only listening to music or only watching TV, or going to nightclubs, you may listen to podcasts about entrepreneurship, you may read new books (especially if you are a writer), or you may even embark on an exercise regimen or spend more time outdoors. These are just a few ideas for starting your transformation from average to outstanding.

COMMANDMENT

2

TELL A STORY

"I'm writing my story so that others might see fragments of themselves."

Lena Waithe, Screenwriter

STORYTIME

If you've ever picked up the Bible, I'm sure you realized very quickly that every time Jesus wanted to get a message across, he told a parable, better known as a story. What makes all stories matter has and always will be the message. Stories involve people and situations that the listener can relate to, and the end of a story must teach us something and, in the best situations, inspire us to become better.

Think of the journeys we have been on with artists Muni Long, Cardi B, 50 Cent, Chief Keef, etc. They all have millions of fans because of their amazing talent. But as fans, we know a significant part of their life's journeys. Their "stories" of obstacles and hardship will continue to inspire generations of musicians across the globe. Says Nigerian-born sensation Mannywellz says, "I'm a DACA recipient here in the USA, which stands for Deferred Action for Childhood Arrivals. It only permits me to stay in the States to work and pay taxes. That's it. I am not a green card holder. I am not a US citizen. So, I can't travel freely and come back to the United States. If I leave, I won't be able to come back. And if I do have to leave, I have to go through a whole process called Advance Parole. And even with Advance Parole, your entry back into the United States isn't always guaranteed. Just depends on whom you meet at the border. So yeah, that's pretty much my life. But through it all, I'm still able to thrive."

There is something in the human spirit that binds us by the heartstrings when we feel connected to someone's story. Your personal story, when told artfully, can open more doors for you than your talent and hard work combined. When telling your story in a way that is honest and inspirational, you can change lives.

Mannywellz speaks about his EP release, entitled *Unwanted*, which tells the story of the pain of being an immigrant in limbo. "The meaning behind the title is that I was just feeling unwanted in the United States because I was too American for Africans, and I was too African for Americans. And on top of that, just being a DACA recipient, not having a green card, and not being a citizen, I just felt unwanted. Throughout that process, I was always reminded that God wants me and I'm here for a purpose. And the first chapter or the first phase is kinda like just making that known through my music and my art."

As unique as your experiences have been, there are millions of people who will resonate with some parts of your life. If you have ever wondered why you had to struggle or were forced to carry so much weight on your shoulders, the reason is that your journey, your pain, and your victories are your greatest gift. Despite the hardships you have been through, you survived. Everything you have been through has created a story that, if properly shared with the world, will open doors that your wildest dreams would have never imagined.

So, if you are guilty of feeling burdened by your past, think of it from a new perspective. Be proud that you have a testimony that will undoubtedly change the lives of millions.

WHAT IS YOUR STORY?

Is it poverty, violence, substance abuse, health issues, fatherlessness, jail, absent mother, or neglect? The list of what makes one's story is as long as there are humans on the earth. My story, for example, was none of those things. My story is a story of entrepreneurialism. As a kid, my father pushed being an entrepreneur on me so much that he made me read business books, and I was only in middle school! I was reading *Rich Dad Poor Dad* (Robert Kiyosaki) and *Who Moved My Cheese (Dr. Spencer Johnson)* and even *Why Should White Guys Have All the Fun?* (Black billionaire Reginald Lewis and Blair S. Walker). Perhaps that is another subconscious reason for my drive to write this book for my people: artists.

Back to the business books that I was required to read—my father wouldn't even take my word for it; he would give me quizzes on the material to make sure I read them and understood them. If I didn't, I was grounded. My childhood was like an entrepreneurship boot camp. I was force-fed. My father is a retired US Army Major, so it all makes sense. My grandmother was also an entrepreneur, owning a whole block on Main Street in Starkville, Mississippi. It was her, in fact, who got me into producing parties, which led me to meet DJs and artists, and that's where the whole music thing began for me. I started out partnering with a producer, Leland Clopton, better known as Big Fruit, who has produced and composed songs for Yo Gotti, Muni Long, K Camp, and Chris Brown. Spending time with those guys in the studio sparked my own talent for songwriting and composing. I realized that I have a knack for music. The rest is our history, which has been a history of independent artists making a lot of money. This book will show you how.

We all have stories that we share that are similar, but it is our outcomes and victories that are so amazingly different. Your career success should be the manifestation of your unique perspective, which should be used in your art, whether you write the most poignant love songs or paint the most beautiful urban landscapes. What you reveal in your work is because of your past. *Use it.*

However, there is an art to delivering your message. The best stories have a strong message, a point, and an intended audience. As the storyteller in all mediums, your objective when crafting a story is to make a clear and meaningful point and to inspire.

For example, I may put my most traumatic experiences in a song and share my emotions to inspire people to keep going no matter what. Another example of meaningful storytelling is when I share my story of being fired from my 9-to-5 job, which forced me to focus on my business, which eventually turned into my primary source of income. What is my consistent message? "Entrepreneurship can save you."

Once you understand your message, your next thought should be about the best way to make your point. With today's attention spans lower than ever, only include the most valid information in your stories as you state your point. You are trying to make friends, but you don't need to overshare because you may lose a lot of the audience with long, drawn-out stories, so share just enough critical information about your experiences that people can feel something that makes any story, no matter the length, unforgettable.

Despite the immigrant crisis in America, Nigerian-born artist, Mannywelllz stays positive. "In my music, I talk about love and God. I talk about life experiences, honestly. I even did a whole project called *Mirage*. It featured only Nigerian artists, which at first wasn't intentional, but when I realized what it was, I thought it was really cool. I talk about my status all the time. I'm very open. I'm very vocal. I've led marches. My story was presented to the Supreme Court when Donald Trump was in office. We were trying to save DACA. My story is one of the reasons why DACA still even exists. Because I was able to share, and the Supreme Court decided to rule in our favor and not remove it. I think this was like 2018, 2019. I worked on a Grammy-winning project, and I've talked about DACA on the Grammys."

YOUR STORY IS WORTH A LOT

Whether you are an artist, author, motivational speaker, or screenwriter, the most successful of these are great storytellers. These people impact their listeners by powerfully sharing their personal journeys. For some, telling your story may require incredible bravery. There is nothing easy about letting the world know your darkest secrets and supposed flaws. However, the bravest storytellers attract the greatest rewards! They do this by telling a story that resonates with listeners but also because of the way they have *interpreted* what has happened to them. And, if I have to add one last nugget, it is that moving stories are great, but the stories that show that the storyteller was able to rise from whatever obstacles they faced and still made it out with grace and wisdom, those are the unforgettable stories.

Lastly, I shouldn't have to say this, but I will. Do not take the word "story" literally. This is NOT an opportunity to dive into fictional narratives. Tell the truth; that is what fans need from you. In these confounding times, the world is hungry for truth.

One of my favorite examples of this is Michelle Obama's book, *Becoming*. Although never known as an author, her book was not only a bestseller; it became a sold-out large stadium tour, a Netflix documentary, and millions of people begging her to run for President! From my perspective, the reason for the amazing success of *Becoming* is the fact that the book told so many unexpected truths about being the wife of the first African American President. That alone makes it inherently compelling. The book shares so many details about the life of the President that we would have never known without her detailing it through the lens of the first Black First Lady. Michelle Obama is so popular because she is without pretense. She is an authentically Black woman who loves music, hip-hop, food, exercise, and all the things that have never been seen in the White House. She is an anomaly, unexpected, and very much lives her life going against the grain of the very formal, conservative backdrop that is the political landscape in the United States. Michelle Obama gave a whole new possibility to what a First Lady can be. Although she is not known as an "artist," she has been artful in her execution of her life and her work. *You can do the same thing.* It's all about being yourself above all else. The world loves to see the "impossible" become possible.

SAME STORY

My story of hanging out with Big Fruit and getting into the music game, of course, was not so simple. Our first big success (Cadillac Don & J-Money's "Inside Peanut Butter, Outside Jelly"), we thought we were big; we went out and lived the big life. But it was extremely short-lived, and we came home broke as a joke. As an entrepreneur already, I paid attention to where all of our money had gone from that short but incredible run. That was my gift, my blessing. My entrepreneurial mind was able to break down what happened. I saw that all of the money was going to the record label. To sum it up, I talked to my partner and said, "Let's start a record label." That's how Family Ties Entertainment started my entrepreneur's journey into the music business.

As you begin to share your story with the world, a few

things will become very clear. Your identity and your message add up to your *brand,* which should be the foundation of all that you are. As an artist, you will find yourself telling your story over and over again. No matter how many times you tell it, there will always be more people who have still never heard it. Be prepared to share your story for the rest of your life, and be even more grateful that you can get to share it with people who want to hear it.

However, the irony of fame is that after you have been successful and touched millions of people with your story and talent, it is still inevitable that the day will come when your journey ends. As an artist, you must be strong enough to understand when your time is over and be wise enough to have given your art the wings it needs to sustain you, even if your "day in the limelight" has ended.

The best examples of this are the countless athletes who have taken their athletic platforms to new places. Although athletes are not considered "artists," they certainly are entertainers. Because of injury or declining performance, the smart ones have gone on to become sportscasters, buy real estate, invest in team ownership, buy pizza and movie theater chains, etc. Don't forget there are many ways to use your platform to stay relevant, even if it's behind the scenes. The entertainment industry is a jungle; only the strong, wise, honest, and consistent survive, and not only do they survive, but they also get to continue adding new chapters to their story.

COMMANDMENT

3

PUT YOURSELF OUT THERE

"Have nuts and be nuts."

Criss Jami, Author, Poet

HAVE NO FEAR

One of the age-old plagues of being an artist is the fear of sharing your art. It's hard to imagine the number of recording artists that I have seen spend years in the studio with hundreds of songs sitting on their hard

> *If you love your shit, you have to show the world that you love it. You have to believe in your art.*
>
> LaRussell, Artist and CEO of Good Compenny

drives, still yet to be heard by the ears of any potential fan or label executive, or even an entrepreneur that could help. How insane is that? But I understand. And, as I talked about in Commandment #1: Tell the Truth, putting your art out there is the most vulnerable thing that you will ever do. I am an artist, too, so I understand. The reason it is so painful is that we have put our all into our work. We have spent countless hours writing it, painting it, rehearsing it, and composing it. You have even had to convince yourself that what you are doing is good and worthwhile. When an artist is still scared to show his art, it may be because he or she has not fully convinced themselves that the work is good. However, I would like to help you undo this fear.

Have you ever gone to a movie, show, reading, play, or concert that you hated? And the person next to you says, "I loved it." And the person next to them says, "I loved the beginning." And the person next to them says, "I hated the beginning but loved the end." And finally, the person across the street says, "I loved it, wouldn't change a thing. "This is just one of a billion scenarios that prove how individual people are. And the fact this illustrates is that there is ALWAYS someone who will see the merit of your work. And so, in order to take the leap of sharing your artwork, you just have to have the mindset that some people will love it and some people will not. And there will be many in between who see something in it but are not totally in love. Even that is GOOD.

What is even more humorous to me is that some of these artists who have never shared their prolific catalog of work, still carry the illusion that they will "make it" one day, without being able to articulate how that can possibly happen. Their vision gets them through when everyone around them is making moves and garnering attention with their art because they did the one thing that this artist (you) hasn't done: *share.* I have seen these artists say that they will be "rich and famous" without ever exposing their work, just keeping it to themselves. I know it sounds ridiculous, but this is a reality for a lot of artists.

Author and screenwriter Steven Pressfield has written several books about the psychological obstacles that curtail creativity. He says in his book *The War of Art*, "The

> *Which is stronger, your dream or your fear?*
>
> J.R. McKee

more scared we are of a work or calling, the more sure we can be that we have to do it."

It is my hope that your dream will always be stronger than your fear. Fear only lasts a few seconds; it ends once you have done the very thing that you feared. A dream that has not been realized can haunt you for a lifetime. If you have been gun-shy about sharing your art with others, I ask you to consider these questions: How much does "making it" matter to you? And what does making it really mean? For artist LaRussell, success means, "Peace. It is being able to look in the mirror and sleep well and be happy with the life that I live."

I pray that you will someday break out of this fear and anxiety because the greatest things in life really are on the other side of fear. Push through fear and stay focused. No, it won't be easy. In fact, every step you take to free yourself from the bondage of fear will feel uncomfortable, but it is the only way to get to where you are headed.

As you sit, bragging to yourself about the hundreds of unheard tracks you have, surely you already know what the bottom feels like. So, today I beg you to stop creating obstacles and emancipate yourself from fear. *You got this.* Think of all the artists that you love, listen to, and admire. They are the same as you. They have a passion and talent, and at some point, they were as terrified as you to share their work. The only difference between you and them at the moment is that they had the courage to push through their fear. And you haven't yet. Today's the day.

YOUR LUCKY DAY

It's a great time to be an artist. There are over 4.66 *billion* potential listeners out there, and no one can stop you from reaching them. We currently live in the streaming era, which means anyone with a smart device can upload their songs and videos and post their poems, paintings, and books anytime and from any place. Today, you can release your music on every streaming platform without even needing to put on your shoes. From the comfort of your home, you could be uploading your newest songs while eating crab legs on the couch. This is my challenge to you. If you would release just one song, scene, painting, or chapter from your book on one social media platform, within hours, you will be able to gauge who responds to your work and why. Or why not. You may be surprised at the positive feedback that you are likely to get from this small experiment that will make a big difference in your future. If you get positive feedback, that should encourage you to share another one and on and on.

If you get negative feedback, that is also positive. Perhaps their unfavorable comment could be something that you never thought of about your work. It may be a quick change to make your work stronger. Maybe they don't like the color choice of your art; perhaps they don't like the references to guns in your lyrics. These are good things to consider. *All feedback is valuable.*

In these exciting, technology-driven times, it is completely illogical to leave your music, paintings, and poems sitting on your hard drive. In fact, building a catalog on streaming platforms plays perfectly into feeding your audience, single by single, EP by EP, and album by album.

Consistency is prominent when you are growing your fan base. Music and other art forms are products, and like all other products, the work must be tested. Your fan base is your ally when it comes to testing your product. When releasing music, remove your anxieties about whether or not the records will be well-received. Your purpose for dropping music is to get an idea for which of your tracks your audience likes best; then, you continue to give them more of what works.

Having a song people don't like helps you get to know your audience better. If they don't like it, they simply won't stream it. It's as simple as that. No one is harmed, and your ego shouldn't be either. If you intend on growing, holding on to your emotions about your art is not the way to do it.

Remember, the energy you put into your work shows the minute people hear, see or read it. If you're not totally confident about your work, people will hear it. Artist Eric Bellinger, who has written with Usher, Chris Brown, Justin Bieber, and Tank, says, "The more you put yourself out there, the more visible you will be."

TALENT SHOW

If you are reading this book, I hope it will be a catalyst for you to believe in the artist that you are and who's ready to step into your light. Although your talent is about 40 percent of the success equation, content is the intangible piece that cements your success. Content is what the public craves, so in order to give "the people what they want," you must be ready to dedicate a majority of your time creating content that will capture the public's attention.

With the drastic shift in the entertainment industry, artists who spend all of their time making art all day tend to forget that the internet and its 4.66 *billion* listeners await them. The internet is your no-fee, all-access chance to debut your brilliance. You must get out there, as scary as it seems. The alternative is far more daunting.

If you have gotten this far in the book, and you are still reluctant, take a deep breath and say to yourself, I have given everything I have to my art. I believe in what I have created. If you can't do that, then you may have to consider that you may not have been totally honest about the work that you are sharing. I have been in this business long enough to understand how easy it is to get swept up in the hype of success, which makes it easy to emulate what you have heard artists that you admire say about their own work. So, I ask you to think long and hard about your artistic journey. Did you give it your all? Was it more work than hanging out? Was it your best? When the answer to all of these questions is yes, then feel confident about what you are delivering. Believe in your work and yourself.

When you believe in your work, then you must put it on display. Create content, and I promise there will be love. Artist and entrepreneur LaRussell follows a model that he has created, which is his guide. He says, "It's called the 10,000 shots theory. For more information, visit: https://goodcompenny.co/products/limitless-the-10-000-shot-theory. If you are not willing to do it 10,000 times, you should quit now. You have to have supreme belief in what you are doing."

A great display of "supreme belief" came from working with Rod Wave on a record titled "Heart On Ice." Rod's voice is a seamless blend of hip-hop, folk, and soul, which makes for an amazing and unique sound. Although Rod is considered a rapper, his tone is almost like folk singer Tracy Chapman, and his emotion is pure rhythm and blues. What if Rod Wave had doubted himself, worrying that his voice was too different? Early in his career, Rod Wave drove up and down Florida, performing at every high school and nightclub he could until he was one of the biggest new hip-hop artists in Florida. Judging from the analytics, "Heart On Ice" was the biggest song on his latest project, so we remixed it with artist Lil Durk, who at the time was a much larger artist than Rod Wave. When we released the remix, nothing major changed until Rod recorded a live performance of himself singing a cappella. That changed everything. When the video hit the internet, it went viral because people were blown away by his compelling voice. There was no auto-tune, no effects or edits-just pure vocals, and it took the internet by storm. This display of talent turned Rod Wave's "Heart on Ice" into a triple platinum record and launched him into superstar status.

As an artist, I say to you, positive things cannot happen in your career if you do not put any positive energy out there. And I'm sure you know that exuding no energy toward your goals is doing nothing, and you will continue to wallow in the same place. Every song you release and every piece of content you post is a direct release of your energy. The more energy you put out there, the more chances you have of that energy coming back to you in the form of success.

If you ever feel stagnant in your career, ask yourself, What energy am I putting out? Consistency is so important because the more you feed the universe on a regular basis, the more it feeds you.

With the internet, miraculous things can happen. Compelled fans can literally make your art go viral overnight, which can very well change your life, but you need to put the energy out first. And, if your first piece is not well-received, it won't ruin your life. You just have to try, try again. It will happen. You have over four billion tries.

One of my first artists, K Camp, was seemingly quiet from 2016 to 2019. Unless you were a core fan, you wouldn't know that he was busy releasing music the entire time. He was consistently putting out energy that returned to him in a major way when, one day in 2019, a little girl on TikTok did a dance to his latest song. When her video went viral, it became the biggest trending dance that TikTok had ever seen. This little girl's dance had the power to thrust K Camp back into the spotlight and earned him his seventh gold-selling record.

How could K Camp have known this little girl would help change his life again? He had no clue. But this opportunity would have never presented itself if he didn't continue to release his music into the world. Consistency is the key. What you desire will make its way to you when it is time. Just keep doing the work. Your time will come.

DON'T TAKE IT PERSONAL

Artists are some of the most creative, talented, and driven human beings on the earth. However, an artist is rarely able to escape their enormous sensitivity. When working with artists, I often find myself telling them not to take criticism or "nos" personally. I know you have heard that a million times before. But what you haven't heard is: Even if it is personal, do not take it personally. I can already see you reading those words and getting defensive and ready to fight.

What you must understand is that taking anything personally fires up our feelings and fuels negative thoughts of revenge and unfriendly competition. Music and entertainment are not the places for that because *art* can never be a competition. Your best art compares to no one else's.

If you intend to have any long-term success, you must stop competing and start collaborating. You've heard the phrase, "Don't hate, participate." Well, it's true. At all levels of this business, collaborating with your peers is greatly beneficial. Whether the artist is more popular than you, equal in popularity to you, or less experienced than you, collaborations can be an excellent bargaining chip for you as you seek new opportunities. This is especially true if you do a collaboration with an artist who is bigger than you. If you do that, it shows audiences that you are on par with the larger artist. For industry executives, it demonstrates your potential, and every executive wants to be the one to discover the next big thing.

Your collaborations with less experienced artists show your audience that you have your finger on the pulse. Your audiences will feel warm towards you, seeing you as a mentor to someone whose talent deserves exposure. This shows that you are a good person and that your ego is firmly in check. It is my prayer that someday you will be the less experienced artist who gets put on. It can only happen if you put yourself out there. Most importantly, *every* collaboration you do will grow you by putting you in front of audiences that you've never been exposed to before. That, alone, is a game-changer.

You may be wondering, How do I go about connecting with other artists to collaborate? Well, it's not easy. You will most likely have to reach out to the artists that you want to collaborate with. I already know the fear of rejection will show up. If you have already made the first step, which is to put your music out there, that will give artists a reference point to listen to your music in their own time. Perhaps, they already have. Make sure whatever music you have put out there is your best work because you never know who's listening. When you go for the big ask, you will be surprised at how many affirmative responses you will get.

Of course, you must prepare for not-so-positive responses, as well. If you get no response or a "no," remember *not to take it personally*. The same no can turn into a yes down the line if you don't react poorly. There are examples of whole careers that have been built on collaborations.

Chicago's Polo G and New York's Lil Tjay were both artists that were buzzing in their hometowns, but neither one of them had found any breakout success. The two got together to collaborate on a song they titled "Pop Out." Little did they know this collaboration would go on to launch both of their careers. Today, as I write this, "Pop Out" is six times platinum.

> *Your career depends on your bravery.*
>
> J.R. McKee

NO DOESN'T ALWAYS MEAN NO

An animal who is free to roam becomes a totally different animal when its back is against the wall. The animal backed into a corner possesses a different strength, a different vigor, and a different mindset. That animal becomes much more dangerous. This is what happens when a person is told no. When a "no" boxes you in a corner, the hunger in you becomes much more dangerous. Your mindset shifts, your energy shifts, and you now have to figure out how to survive. This is why in many cases, nos are the best thing that can happen to you.

I owe a big part of my career to a no. If it wasn't for labels turning down our first artist, Tha Joker, I would have never discovered that I could make money independently. I was the first person to put a mixtape on iTunes, which opened the door for independent hip-hop to thrive in the digital age. That door was

> *Nos force you to think smarter and dig deeper.*
>
> J.R. McKee

only opened because someone told me no.

Nos can be turned into yeses. A lot of times, people are not seeing your vision early on, and so you may have to take control of the situation by going out there and turning your vision into reality. The people who said no

> *In business, 99 percent of the time, "nos" mean "not yet."*
>
> J.R. McKee

will be surprised and maybe even regretful. People don't believe what's in your head; they only believe what's in your hand. The crazy part is that most of the time, once they're ready to say yes, you've already outgrown needing them. But it's quite possible that you would never have grown to where you are had they not said no. So, value your nos because one day, you will be forever grateful. Remember, most opportunities need to be created. And you are a creator, right?

I'm so grateful that we couldn't get a record deal. We met with all the labels, and nobody would sign us. We were from Mississippi, and there were no stars in Mississippi at the time, and we didn't have any experience. It was just us. The point is that is the reason why I always thought outside of major labels. I would have never been able to build the type of wealth I have been able to build if I had been tied up with the label. I would be nowhere near where I am right now.

J.R. McKee

COMMANDMENT

4

IDENTIFY & ENGAGE YOUR AUDIENCE

"I've learned that people will forget what you said, people will forget what you did, but people will never forget how you made them feel."

Maya Angelou, Poet, and Civil Rights Activist

THE DEFINITION OF A FAN

We all understand that in order to be a thriving artist, let alone a superstar, you need an audience a fan base. However, most people with dreams of succeeding in the industry skip over learning what a fan actually is; by skipping over this knowledge, they never end up with any actual fans.

My definition of a fan is someone who directly relates to you and your message. They either relate to where you are, have been where you are, or want to be where you are or where you are headed. Basically, someone who has made a personal connection with you through your art, your story, your content, and the most powerful tool of them all, your engagement.

Having a strong fan base is more about having support for the long haul rather than fanfare. Fanfare simply refers to behaviors: applause, standing ovations, cheering, and screaming. Those behaviors are not sustainable. Fanfare is what can convince an artist that they have a huge following when, in reality, they just have a room full of people clapping. And these same people will be the first to leave you when they find another hit to clap for.

When making your way to the top, be aware of fans who actively support you and your music. Your art not only resonates with them, but they actually see themselves in you. You inspire them, and they want to stand in solidarity with you for the long haul. When you are creating, think only of those who love you. Put the haters out of your mind. There will always be detractors, but you must remember that an artist is in the business of sending out love. Don't let haters near you.

Artists need support for their full body of work, not just the one that is on the radio or up in the art gallery. The way to get this kind of support is to make sure your audience knows you intimately. As an artist, you are ever-evolving. And so having a solid fan base allows you the freedom and flexibility to let your art grow. You may be known for ballads, but you may want to mix it up a little and put out some dance music. You may be known for abstract art, and then you have decided to go into collage and mixed media. You need a true fan base that understands the shifts because they understand your life. With constant activity (social media, homemade videos of you sharing what you are feeling or experiencing in your life), your true fans will be there to support you when you have made an artistic shift. Of course, when an artist makes significant changes to their art, they run the risk of "fans" saying negative things. However, because you have skillfully curated a loyal following, you can be confident that your fan base will support the work no matter what the critics say. And the best part is that by having art that is evolving, you are poised to attract all new fans that will also need to be courted by your constant engagement. It's a win-win.

WHAT IS YOUR BRAND?

I am sure you hear the word "brand" being thrown around a lot. Initially, a brand simply meant the company that was behind the product (a name or logo). It was an advertising/marketing term that didn't carry the weight that "branding" carries now. I think that the easiest explanation of what a brand has come to mean is what that company stands for. Think of Mercedes Benz. It immediately evokes luxury, wealth, and excellence. However, Honda evokes safety and reliability. One is aspirational, and the other is "common" (accessible). A brand asks the consumer: Which do you want to be? Brands do best when they evoke a strong emotional response. Car manufacturers use famous actors and musicians to show whom their campaign wants to attract; perfume brands create fantastical sultry images of romance, speaking directly to the demographic who buys into those fantasies. Marketers hope that the elaborate and costly visual positioning translates to audiences what owning the brand can do for its audience's profile and overall happiness.

There was a time when large corporations only advertised the details of their cars: 4-wheel drive, low gas mileage, powerful engine, etc. Then, marketing became more sophisticated, and marketers were looking at demographics (where people live) and psychographics (how they think). When marketers started speaking directly to the audiences' hopes and dreams for themselves, the landscape of car marketing changed forever. Those same principles can be applied to you and your art.

Who are you? What do you stand for? Are you an environmentalist? A Christian? A feminist? A family man?

An athlete/fitness buff? Soccer mom? Self-appointed chef? Are you a vegan or vegetarian? Are you a cancer survivor? Believe it or not, these things matter when determining your brand. People are drawn to artists that have things in common with them. Who you are as a human being is the foundation of your brand. While you intend to share your art with the world, what they really want is the human behind the art. Who you are as a person has become much more important to being an artist than ever before. If you can make people fall in love with you as a person, your art is almost guaranteed to be appreciated. A fan can like a song and not care at all about the artist who made it, but the opposite is almost never true. Think of Rihanna, whose career has expanded from being a musician to having a fashion empire due to the love of her fans. Her Fenty brand has expanded to lingerie, perfume, and even makeup. All supported by her loyal fan base.

In order to solidify one's brand, it is important to identify at least three key aspects of yourself that are a part of everything you do. I call these brand keys. I believe that everything you do has to stem from the tenets of your brand. When you are engaging in activities that are off-brand, you are harming your brand. Staying true to your brand means that it is easier to find you and match you with others with the same belief systems. One of your brand keys can't be vegan and committed to saving the planet while fans see you chowing down on ribs and smoking. You have to stay on-brand and look for opportunities that fit your brand. The things you identify with most are the keys to building loyal audiences. For example, my brand keys are 1) entrepreneurialism, 2) my mastery of streaming, and 3) being a family man. My fans know these three things about me, and my loyal fans either have these same passions, or they aspire to at least one of the keys. My followers are inspired by seeing a happy family with a loving husband, wife, and children, all while being in the entertainment world, which is often hard to do. And you will notice that everything I do is related to one of those three things, including writing this book. This book fits into my brand keys because it offers wisdom for aspiring artists by offering ways for artists to take control of their careers by tapping into the key ingredients needed to build successful careers. I am *all about* inspiring artists to take control of their destinies by monetizing their talent in creative ways that do not allow the art industries to swallow them up and spit them out, which is what happens to many artists who are uneducated on the business.

Once you have chosen your brand keys, everything you release should be centered around them, and that is how your audience will find you and connect with you. Stand for something and be firm when identifying your brand, always staying on brand. And because this may be your first time thinking about it, they can change. But this is the time to start working on it. Write with a pencil. You may change them many times before you land on the three things that really resonate and that you know you can live by.

List your three brand keys here:

_____   _____   _____

Now that you see your three potential brand keys on paper, do they resonate with you as something you're willing to build a career on? An immediate answer is not needed, but I offer you the space to think about it.

You are Seen

When you begin to share your story with the world, something strange happens; people you've never met will engage with you with likes and/or comments. Their interaction should comfort

> *If you live by the applause, you'll die by the boos.*
>
> J.R. McKee

you in knowing that you are seen, heard, and felt. There is no such thing as a stranger. There are only fans that you have not yet met.

Fans come when your story resonates with them. With eight billion people in the world and five billion actively engaged online, millions will identify with who you are and where you are in life. In the beginning, do not worry about identifying your audience, just tell your story and let them find you.

Every day, billions of people go online and search explorer pages, hashtags, and shared content for things they enjoy. The quantity of those that find and engage with you may start off small, but the number of people engaging with you isn't the most important factor. *Who* engages with your content will set you on your journey to becoming the artist you envision yourself to be.

The Streaming Era is the Easiest Era to Identify Your Audiences

There is something beautiful about knowing who your allies are. When you share your message, you are basically asking, Who's with me? And thanks to data and analytics, you can have the answer.

Data is king in today's internet world. Data is now valued even more than real estate. Every social media platform and every streaming platform collects data. So, every move your fans make is recorded and documented. Now, while you do not have the luxury of owning this data, these platforms share some of the information they collect from your account activity or otherwise make it available for you to use. This collected information is known as analytics. These analytics are the road map to your success. They tell you who is listening and watching, where they are listening and watching from, and when. As you begin to tell your story and put your energy out via music and content, everyone attracted to it will be documented by these analytics. The analytics will paint a picture of who your core audience is going to be. What used to take intuition, research hours, and many weeks on the road is now at your fingertips on each platform's dashboard. This is today's version of demographics and psychographics. It is powerful and somewhat amazing.

Of course, the connection between your art and social media is enormous. Analytics itself is a new thriving industry. Music executive, Bryan Calhoun, has been ahead of the curve of this discipline for a long time. As a former record executive and known guru for helping artists get the most out of their technology-based presence, he has developed websites and social media accounts and, most of all, set up the analytics so that artists can track their sales and streams, as well as understand their audience better. Calhoun's book, *The Music Business Toolbox*, is currently being used in several music industry courses at several universities. In the section on analytics, Calhoun writes, "There are some very nice-looking data dashboards out there, which make it possible for you to access an enormous amount of information about your music's social resonance. But here is a warning: Always ask yourself, What can I do with this information? Does the data help you route a tour or reveal what the next single is or match you with similar artists? Have you discovered your music is popular in Brazil or that you're a hit with teens? As you discover things, think about what is possible to take action on, and then figure out if it's affordable and wise to do....for YOU."

BULLSEYE

To take advantage of the plethora of resources to track music, specifically, check out these valuable resources:

Musicbusinesstoolbox.com

And for analytics platforms:
https://chartmetric.com
https://soundcharts.com
https://www.crowdtangle.com
https://artists.apple.com
https://artists.spotify.com
https://artists.amazon.com
https://www.ampplaybook.com
https://studio.youtube.com

> *One of the most valuable pieces of data is how many recipients took action, whether that was clicking on a link to watch a video or clicking on a link to buy a ticket to a show. Review your analytic data carefully to see if there's something you can learn about your message from how readers reacted to it.*
>
> Bryan Calhoun, *Author,* The Music Business Toolbox

GETTING TO KNOW YOU

Once you know who your people are, you can find more of them. As an artist, in the beginning, you speak your message to whoever is in earshot, but once you've identified your target audience, it's time to pick up the bullhorn and direct it to those who are listening and everyone else like them. Everything you do, your target audience should be aware of. For example, if you discover that your message really resonates with college students, then you can begin to target them directly. Find out what pages college students follow on social media so that you can post to those pages and what type of visuals college students are attracted to so you can make sure your visuals are more attractive to them. You'll even be able to understand through analytics what time college students watch the most music videos, which is the time that you should post your videos.

Yes, you are an artist above all else, but as you start to see your art as your business, understand that you are a brand first, and it is crucial that you stay on brand. Learn to fit your lifestyle into your audience's world. Social media is the current TV network of choice, and your brand needs to be on-air constantly. Every post you make will be viewed as the thoughts and views of your brand. Therefore, every post you make should be with intent. Each post should be intended to serve and grow your brand.

Know How to Work with Your Streaming Cycle

A Streaming Cycle is a strategy that I developed to work more effectively in scheduling artists' releases according to their analytics. Imagine you put out a new song, and your song is being actively listened to by your fan base for a certain period of time: your streaming cycle. When I say actively listening, I mean waking up in the morning with the song on their mind; the fan initially plays it every morning while they get ready for work, for example. Then Beyoncé or anyone else puts out a new song, and they switch to that in the mornings. The analytics can give you a great gauge on when this normally happens for you; when your fans stop actively listening, that's the end of your streaming cycle. For most artists, the streaming cycle is between two to six weeks. You can see the active listening data when studying your analytics. If a song is being actively streamed for three weeks, on the third week, you need to put out a new song before they switch again and forget you. I teach all about this in my streaming business master classes available at sharedinformation.co.

GET ENGAGED

From the day you launch your "TV network" on social media posting intentional content, people you never imagined will start stumbling into your world. They'll show up in your likes, comments, and your direct messages, and as they show up, it's your number one job to keep them hooked. Engage them and reply to their comments and their DMs. Go to their pages and like and comment on what they have going on. Express a real interest because that's how you build genuine relationships. And if this sounds daunting and time-consuming, just look at it as the "paperwork" part of your business. It's tedious, but it has to be done. Your art is your business, right? These small acknowledgments of each and every fan that shows interest in your art or posts will pay off in the long run.

Don't ever make the mistake of believing you are more important than your fans. Many artists at concerts and award shows get on stage and say, "I'd be nothing without my fans," and it's true. And no matter how successful you become, you will never be able to make a living in entertainment without the support of your fans. Those who feel engaged by you, even with a smile emoji or just a fire emoji left on their page by you, will go a long way in building your audience.

The beautiful truth about engaging your fans is that it creates a sense of reciprocity. If Drake leaves a comment on your page today and drops an album tomorrow, I bet the only thing you would listen to is his new album, but why? It's because you would instantly feel connected to Drake. He created a personal interaction. A superstar like Drake reaching out to you begins the process of reciprocity. The least you can do is listen to his new album, and you'd do it with pride. Every human being who feels engaged by another creates a reciprocal relationship. Whether you realize it or not, your small gestures that engage with your fans will do a lot of work for you. The lucky recipient of your gesture is almost obligated to talk about you to others, share your music, and share your post. They believe it is part of their new "relationship," and it is one of the greatest ways to create new fans. This is what a small "like" can do for you. The more people you engage, the more fans you create, and the more fans you create, the more fans those fans create. *This* is how you build your fan base.

Tap into Other Audiences

When it comes to your music or life story, no matter how unique your sound is, there will always be someone who came before you. Someone has already paved the way for your sound, which means there is already a fan base that exists for you. When you release music, use this knowledge to your advantage. Share your music using the hashtags of those who came before you, engage with their fan pages, and target their bases when advertising. If they love that artist, there is a strong chance that they will love you, too. Whatever your sound may be, fans of all sounds do exist; you may be surprised by who they are and where they are. So, when releasing your music, go with your data, not your gut.

COMMANDMENT

5

SELL EARLY

"I make money from touring and selling merchandise, and I honestly believe if you put effort into something and you execute properly, you don't have to necessarily have to go through traditional ways."

Chance the Rapper

TRAINING DAY

How can an artist train their fans to be consumers? And what happens if you don't? Imagine having one of the hottest songs in the country, you roll down your window at a red light and hear all the cars playing your song, and when you look over at a kid's phone screen, they are watching your music video. This is the type of traction and influence that artists dream of.

However, digital streaming is only the first step. Next, it's time for your team to prepare for the drop of your first piece of merchandise that's guaranteed to sell out because everyone is in love with your record. The day comes, the T-shirts are posted on your site, and the shopping cart is all set up. And nothing happens. No one is buying.

I've seen this happen numerous times to some of the most successful artists. Why? Because their fans weren't trained to be consumers. On the flip side of that coin, I've watched artists that have never had a hit record sell millions in merchandise because they trained their fans to be consumers from day one. When you're building a fan base, you must get them in the habit of supporting you financially. By being loyal fans, they have already shown their dedication and their willingness to support your dreams. Believe it or not, loyal fans get great satisfaction from being able to say that they were first to get your T-shirt and first to carry your backpack. When your fans are wearing your merchandise, they are actually advertising your brand. The merchandise is further proof that they are part of your squad, and that goes a long way for fans and artists alike.

From the beginning, me and my team try to work with our first one hundred fans, trying to get them prepared to invest in us. When you are working with a finite number like that, it's easier to create offers. For example, if you have one hundred fans, ten T-shirts is a great first offer. This gives a feeling of urgency, and people will be excited to "prove" their loyalty to you by being among the first ten to purchase. The next time you may have something else that you sell for fifty dollars. If you do this every few months, your fans become accustomed to purchasing more than music from you. What's most important is that you connect some meaning to the merchandise you sell: "This is our first concert T-shirt," or, "As a kid, I had one backpack that I took everywhere. It was my only possession. Now, I am selling only twenty backpacks to my biggest fans." Your fans have to feel like the item means something to you. This is another time when your personal story comes in handy.

At the beginning of your career, merchandise is another way of connecting with your fans. You want them to have something special, something tangible, to show how big of a fan they are and how important you are to them. The truth is for it to be important to them, it has to be important to you. Don't make the mistake of slapping your logo on any old thing and calling it "merch." You have to be able to give meaning to the merchandise that you sell. Your fans need to know why this purchase is so important that there are only twenty-five shirts available. Remember, in the early days of your success, you may be working with a limited number of loyal fans to sell to. It is very wise to sell extremely limited and rare merchandise to these fans. This will help accomplish your goal of training your fans to be consumers with a sense of urgency. Believe me; they want to make the ultimate statement: I was here first.

BUILD YOUR OWN DATABASE; PLATFORMS COME AND GO

Social media has become a lifeline for millions of people who rely on it to communicate, get news, share pictures and videos, and know what's going on with millions of people just like them. The unfortunate news is that these platforms come and go. Just like anything, nothing lasts forever. As an artist, if you have utilized one of these platforms to collect your fan base's data, if something happens, like Elon Musk buys the platform, for example, you may lose your list as the platform may go through changes due to new management. If the platform goes away, so do your followers, and if you lose your followers, you lose your ability to sell.

Whether it be an email list or cell phone list, or both, you must invite your fans to join *your* list. It's easy to do when you offer them incentives like exclusive content or early drops if they join. By creating your own database, you can be assured that it won't go anywhere unless you delete it. Your personal database gives you direct access to your followers. Once you have invited them to "join," future sellouts of whatever you decide to sell are almost guaranteed. Now, of course, in creating a database that is officially yours, you must not only offer them incentives; you must also continuously engage them and entertain them with new material.

STREAM TEAM

Artists often make the mistake of assuming because they put music out, they have done their job. I want you to put out music that people will listen to, but more importantly, I want your fans to care about you as much as the music. As an artist who has spent thousands of hours perfecting their craft, you didn't create the art just to produce something; you did it because it has meaning. And it must continue to.

This is where your database comes in handy. Tell your fans why this music is important to you; what's the story behind it? Did you write this song on the day of your first child's birth? Was this the first painting you ever completed, and it hung in your mother's home for fifteen years? You can not only share stories about your art and merchandise, but you can also go one step further and invite fans into your creative process. Posting videos of rehearsals done in your living room or at the studio allows your fans the ultimate access to you and your music, but even more significantly, they have access to your creative process. Once you do this, your fans will be forever invested in you and your work. Needless to say, if your fans were a part of your living room rehearsal or studio session, they will indubitably share it with others. Of course, it is yours, but it is now theirs, too. This is how you convert your fans into a stream team.

THE MAGIC TOUCH

In the post-Covid era, we are back outside. The internet, streaming, and online concerts have done the best they could to alleviate the loss of connection. However, as magical as the internet is, it can never replace human touch. As Covid restrictions are lifting, live concerts are back, and fans are getting the magic of the live experience once again. So now more than ever, the strongest connection will always come from in-person encounters.

Make sure your team is aware of what it takes to make live appearances the best they have ever been. Will it be a meet and greet after the concert for your local fan base? Is it a chance to take a picture with you? The world is a crazy place, and although we had to learn how to live remotely, we are now learning how to be together again. People feel most connected to you when they can feel your emotions and energy and when they can feel your love of your craft. For those more introverted artists, these years where you couldn't go out may have felt like a relief. But now, it is showtime, and you have to be ready. Get your game face on and go meet the people who have made it all possible.

COMMANDMENT

6

TRIAL & ERROR

*"Progress through trial and error
depends not only on making trials,
but on recognizing errors."*

Virginia Postrel, Author

Take it to Trial

A successful person is one who has failed the most. I'll repeat that. A successful person is one who has failed the most. It is so true! The more you fail, the more you understand what works and what doesn't. The artist with the most comprehensive understanding of the situation is the most likely to eventually succeed.

The only way to get this understanding is by trial and error. Thomas Edison, the inventor of the light bulb, famously failed ten thousand times before getting the light bulb right. But he didn't say he failed ten thousand times; he said he found ten thousand ways that didn't work. Don't give up. Experience your errors to earn your stripes.

As an artist, there's no need to guess what people think about your work. In the age of social media, you can get instantaneous feedback. The second you post, your fans will be there to tell you exactly what they think. The majority of your content may receive lackluster engagement, and that is totally fine because you are focused

> *The artist is grounded in freedom. He is not afraid of it. He is lucky. He was born in the right place. He has a core of self-confidence, of hope for the future. He believes in progress and evolution. His faith is that humankind is advancing, however haltingly and imperfectly, toward a better world.*
>
> Steven Pressfield, Author, The War of Art

on learning exactly what does not work. If a new piece of your content gets much more engagement than you're used to getting, that content becomes your "gold," and you should use it as your yellow brick road to future victories.

OUTSIDE LOOKING IN

Do you ever look at your favorite artist and think, Man, they have it all figured out? Well, I can tell you right now that they don't. Just the journey of making art in and of itself is the utmost example of trial and error. It may be hard to believe that a song that you didn't love and may not have even considered for release, only luck (or God) would have it that it ends up on the album and becomes a single. It turns out millions of people love it, and *it wasn't even supposed to be released.* Imagine that. And, when it became a hit, everyone, artists and executives alike, shook their heads and bathed in the glory. It never came up again why someone doubted it in the first place. That is no longer relevant. What is relevant, the only thing that matters, is the fact that it was a hit.

It also happens the other way: the song that you believed in with all of your might was released as a single and performed poorly. Remember, the very act of creating is always trial and error. A piece of art's success is always subject to many intangibles, such as current events, timing, shifting societal attitudes, etc. As Grammy award-winning songwriter Blu June of the hitmaking team Nova Wav said, "You can have a hit song and give it to the wrong artist."

We've already discussed that just the idea of sharing your art feels risky and frightening, yet it's the most important thing that you will ever do. Yes, after you have built up the courage, there is an even worse aspect: You'll never know what the response will be. As a creative myself and one who works closely with artists every day, I only can offer you this: Trial and error allows you to understand and measure the effectiveness of your art in the way it resonates with audiences.

Everything that an artist puts out starts as a trial, and they pray and cross their fingers that it's not an error. But sometimes it is. Imagine, back in the day, an artist's trepidation when they had already received their advance and all recording studio fees had been paid, and the day had come that they must go to the label and present the album. Believe me; those artists had the exact same feeling you did when you were riddled with fear about putting your song out there. Times may have changed, but the artist's fears are always the same.

Artists can also experience the riskiness of trial and error with their messaging. The same concept applies when you are trying a new approach, tempo, or style with a song, which is the same as trying out something new to say to your audience. Sometimes saying things that you have never said before can be risky because you can't possibly know how the audience will react. This happened with Kanye West when he released the album *Yeezus*, an edgy rock collection with stark electronics and controversial lyrics, including songs entitled, "New Slaves" & "I Am a

God." The album was poorly received by his core audience, which is why he did not continue down the hard rock path. His audience loves him for what he has always done best. Because of his reputation for making groundbreaking hip-hop, it was not difficult for him to recover.

An artist should be careful not to offend. This is a game of getting a ride-or-die fan base. It is your job to stay abreast of the news in order to constantly know the pulse of what is happening in the world around you because shifting attitudes or a message that can be considered hate towards other communities can tarnish your career, robbing you of credibility and money. Remember, you are an artist. You are in the love business.

Did you know that global megastar Rihanna has twenty-five top ten singles? Did you also know that Rihanna has actually released *fifty-two* singles? That means more than half of her singles could be considered failures. But do you even care now that you have fallen in love with the twenty-five chart toppers that she has had? Of course not. Just remember that Rihanna could *not* have had twenty-five successful hits if she didn't *try* fifty-two times.

With all this talk of trying new things, I just say to you that you must be strategic in building a fan base that will understand your choices and defend them, whether it is artistically or your messaging. This brings us back to your brand and your three brand keys. This is another time to think about these foundational concepts that are what you, your music, and your career will stand on. Have they changed since you have read more? If so, write them down again.

_____ _____ _____

Your brand is a work in progress.

Here is another example of how trial and error can be exciting and lucrative. It seems that record labels are pairing together artists of different eras and asking them to collaborate. As strange as it may seem, it has happened successfully with artists like thirty-seven-year-old Lady Gaga collaborating with the late ninety-six-year-old Tony Bennett or seventy-five-year-old Sir Elton John pairing successfully with twenty-seven-year-old Dua Lipa and forty-year-old Britney Spears. Their collaborations proved valuable as they made old hits come alive again for a new generation of listeners.

I wasn't there, but I can imagine that folks were quite surprised with the idea of thirty-seven-year-old alternative artist Lady Gaga being asked to work on ninety-six-year-old Tony Bennett's songs, which are now considered "standards" because they have been popular across multiple generations.

The idea of getting them together for one meeting, much less a song or two or even a full concert, could have been a disaster, but because the two of them are each a master in their own right, it worked artistically, but it also wowed audiences from all ages to witness this amazing collection of immeasurable talent coming together.

It is often worth it to try new things, even if they seem outrageous, unthinkable, and infeasible. This brings us back to the ride-or-die fan base you are working to cultivate. Those are people who won't let you down even when you try something unthinkable. With art, nothing is unthinkable, and everything is possible.

When Trying Something New, Be Inspired but Never Compare

After reading this commandment, some of you may be itching to try something new because perhaps the one thing you

> *If it's confusing at first, that's a good sign.*
>
> D'Angelo

have always done is not working so well. I have just given you several examples of artists taking risks, venturing into unchartered water. Now you may be thinking, I want to try something new. Your desire to try something new is admirable.

I will say it again: Do you. Never compare yourself to anyone. When you look left or right at another person's journey, you have no idea what that person is going through or what they have been through to arrive

> *The thief of all joy is comparison.*
>
> J.R. McKee

at where they are. You cannot recreate another artist's journey. Those examples that I gave could have been artists who are in the same position you are, wanting to add something new and unexpected to their music. So, when you read this and try to come up with something that could be a trial and lead to a victory, I ask you to go inward and think of things that have influenced you on your art journey. Think of music or art that inspired you as a child. Even think back to music or art that you hated as a child. Listen to it now; you may have a whole new understanding of it. Let you and your life experiences and exposures lead you to the place where you can experiment with your sound. And then I say, *Go for it.*

Focus on yourself and yourself only. Your journey is about growing. It is easier to go forward when you are already moving. Even if you have been working on music and nothing has happened yet, you are at least moving forward. Measure your success by your own growth. Not someone else's.

COMMANDMENT

7

LAWYER UP

"Without law, men are beasts."

Maxwell Anderson, Author, Poet, Lyricist

How Do You Find the Right Lawyer?

Each profession has its good and bad apples. A good lawyer is one that is honorable and skillful, professional and pleasant to work with. An extraordinary lawyer should be all of those things but also possesses an exceptional network.

Besides knowing the law and protecting their clients, an exceptional lawyer is also a dealmaker, and because of their network, they have an easier time making deals on your behalf with people they already know who can help your career. In this business, a deal is likely to be on the table because your lawyer was able to call and put you on someone's radar.

Lawyers also have to be current and in the mix because deal structures, like most things in life, are constantly changing. Industry information is being consumed at a much higher rate because of the internet. Artists are educating themselves, so more deals are getting done, and because of educated artists like you, the deals are becoming fairer than they have ever been.

When you are looking for a lawyer, you want someone who is savvy and knowledgeable about what the most current terms to date are so you don't get stuck in a contract structure from years ago.

When speaking with a lawyer, ask them who they currently represent. Listen for people in your current field of art; you want someone who knows the arena in which you will exist. For instance, you do not want to hire a lawyer that specializes in health cases or car accidents to represent your entertainment legalities. You also want someone experienced and currently practicing law. Stay away from attorneys who have been off of the scene or practiced years prior.

Lawyers normally work in firms, so even if you can't afford the top lawyer, you can work with associates at their firm and reap the benefits of the firm's legal connections. Whatever you do, get representation.

From my perspective, a lawyer is the very first person you should add to your team, even before a manager, because every step of your journey will require a lawyer, from endorsements and shows, to record deals and even management contracts.

No final decisions, *especially signed contracts,* should ever be done without legal representation and approval from an attorney with experience in your chosen art's industry. Entertainment and sports attorney, Leron Rogers says, "If an artist doesn't understand the nuances in industry norms, the right attorney can be an advocate in the creative process. The skill and value of a music attorney is they have the experience to articulate the value of an artist's work to the label. Labels always want the artists for the cheapest amount, but even the artists don't know that they are worth a million dollars."

Your best bet at finding a good lawyer is by referral, asking other artists in the business about their lawyer and how their experience is going. If you are referred by another creative who is not in music, their lawyer may be able to guide you to someone who is.

Rule #1:

The first thing artists should understand is that their art is intellectual property, which means that what you have created belongs to YOU. Protection of your intellectual property in music is called a copyright. Your art, IP (intellectual property), is extremely valuable and must be protected from other artists, crooked managers, money-hungry publishers, and ruthless music executives. And, if you are ever in a fight to own or reclaim the rights to your original art (or idea), an attorney will always be your best defense. These types of negotiations and disputes cannot be done without industry-specific legal expertise.

When asked what is the most common mistake that he encounters with young recording artists, Rogers says, "When you have young artists so anxious to get on, they throw caution to the wind and will sign whatever. Young artists will sign a contract that is unfair (inappropriate) for where they are in their career. These contracts often ask for too many rights that the artist didn't have to give up before they've even had a hit. When they do this, they have lost leverage."

IT'S ALL ABOUT CONTRACTS

Contracts are agreements between two or more parties that are upheld by law once signed. In music, as well as other areas of entertainment, I've seen many people fail to understand the language in contracts yet sign their names anyway. But how can you agree to something you don't understand? The sad answer is once you've signed the contract, it doesn't matter if you understood it or not. There are thousands of cases of this that increased astronomically when hip-hop started to emerge in the early '70s. It seemed there was an understanding that "street kids" would not understand the legalese in formal contracts and would sign anything out of desperation to get out of "the hood."

To further support my belief in entrepreneurism in the arts, I suggest that you read this article titled "Just Say No to 360s: Hip-Hop's Claim of Economic Exploitation." Author Christopher Vito writes, "Forbes magazine reported that Strange Music's Tech N9ne made an estimated 7.5 million dollars in 2012, which was more than mainstream artists 50 Cent, Mac Miller, and Rick Ross (Greenburg 2013). They wrote that Tech N9ne attributes a large part of his success to building a strong fan base without the help of a major record label. His business model, which includes a deal with Isolation Network's independent distribution company Fontana, ultimately produces high-profit margins with relatively low cost, as noted in "Crybaby" (2008). Tech N9ne's success has traditionally been seen as an exception to the case, as indie labels have traditionally owned only 10-15% of the market share (Day 2011). Yet recent studies have shown that this number is steadily increasing as independents now make up as much as 30% of the market share (Moore 2013)."

So many early hip-hop artists suffered these terrible deals that it has become common knowledge how important an attorney is to an artist's bottom line. However, as an artist and entrepreneur, it is obvious that despite having an attorney, you should be well-schooled on these items for yourself.

All that being said, that's why you should *never* sign anything that your lawyer hasn't looked over and thoroughly explained to you. And if you still don't understand, you should ask as many questions as you have to. I'm sure you've heard enough entertainment horror stories to understand the urgency of my words.

The fact that you're reading this book suggests that you possess enough knowledge and have a large enough entrepreneurial spirit to be on the other side of this battle, the winning side, where you and your lawyers are driving the terms. Being on this side of the equation when it comes to contracts will save your life and your assets. Contracts hold all parties accountable for what they have promised to provide, whether it be an artist, their manager, or their label, making sure that all parties perform their side of the deal.

Another thing that is crucial to know about contracts is that most contracts are not short-term. Normally, contracts have you engaged with the other party for long periods of time, often years. Life is short, and your prime is even shorter, so the last thing you want is to be tied up in a bad deal for years out of your life.

I have heard many new artists say, "I can't afford to hire a lawyer out of the gate," or, "I haven't made any money yet." Somehow, the music business is the only business that people think they can enter without any financial investment. All businesses require a plan and capital to get started. The entertainment business is no different, and the one cost you can't afford to cut is securing a lawyer.

Since lack of money is often a major concern, I asked Leron Rogers if he could break down the costs that are associated with hiring a lawyer. Now, these numbers that he offers are just a range to give you a ballpark sense of what you can expect. Under normal circumstances, entertainment law is mostly about contracts between the artist and various supporting entities, which could be a record label, a publishing house for authors, or a gallery or agent for visual artists.

According to Rogers, the costs are "depending on what you are getting reviewed." For example, a management agreement for an independent artist could be anywhere from $1,000-$2,500, and for a more established entity, $2,500-$7,500 for a deal that is perhaps more complicated.

Most attorneys charge 5 percent of the deal they negotiate. Often, the attorney can get the label to pay this as an additional advance out of the album fund. Sometimes, on an ongoing basis, the attorney is also entitled to 5 percent of ongoing revenues, which is not necessarily in the contract. This stipulation would appear in a *letter of direction* that is mutually agreed upon by the artist and the attorney.

That may sound crazy since it is unknown what the revenue will be for the artist. Needless to say, those kinds of deals are reserved for superstar artists whose revenue is nearly guaranteed based on their global platform and past success.

Rogers goes on to explain that management agreements between artists and managers can also get complicated. Suppose an artist hears from his prospective manager that he wants to charge 40 percent of the artist's revenue when in actuality, the industry norm is 20 percent. If that scenario occurs, the attorney has the task of sorting out this disparity. This means that it would take longer, which means the lawyer fees will be more than originally estimated because there is a snag with the management agreement. This kind of thing happens all of the time, and the reasons are varied. Perhaps the manager is new and unknowledgeable about industry standards, or perhaps the artist and manager have a history that includes money being owed to the manager. Or the manager knows how high maintenance this artist is and feels that a higher fee is warranted. The possible scenarios are endless, but this is just a rudimentary example of how a straightforward transaction can get complicated. And every complication adds to the cost.

If you are still aspiring to get a major label deal, it is

important to understand that labels require distribution rights, meaning they earn percentages of the sales and streams of your projects. In addition, labels have a say-so about images, timelines, visuals, and releases. Simply put, you give up a lot of your creative freedom because often label executives know "what sells," even if it is different from what you want to release. Because of the money that has changed hands, contractually, you have relinquished some of your creative desires for your project. That is something to seriously consider when deciding whether to get a traditional record label deal or to stay independent.

How many times have you heard about your favorite artists feeling betrayed and upset with music labels behind "bad deals"? Many artists, no matter how successful, work hard at recording music, and the joy is taken from them when their projects cannot be released in a timely manner to the fan base whom they have cultivated over decades. One of the most public examples of this was with Prince, who spent the last decade of his life battling his record label.

Every artist that I have ever met has his or her own philosophy of how to manage their business. It is always my hope that young artists turn their art into a business that can sustain them for a long time. LaRussell is one of my favorite examples of a true artist who is also a thriving entrepreneur with his company, Good Compenny. His philosophy is very different when it comes to his art, and I respect the way he thinks. When it comes to his business, LaRussell says, "I live by the principle, stay out of court. If they want to sue me, I will give it to them. I don't want to deal with the energy. Just do good business and stay out of court."

I wish it were that simple. But there are several important things about this statement that need to be acknowledged. Because he is independent, LaRussell has significantly more authority over his art than artists who are tied to a record label, so he has the freedom to adopt his own standards for operation. His independence allows him to have this attitude about his art and how he uses it and how others use it or not. As an artist with obligations to a record label or independent distribution company, your autonomous dealings, promises, favors, etc., could get you in legal trouble.

I know that LaRussell would not over-promise things he cannot honor or utilize other's art without permission and would not breach a contract by not showing up to an agreed-upon event, etc. Being in control of all aspects of your work keeps you in control. It is important to glean two important things that LaRussell is saying here. Being wrapped up in legal entanglements is not only time-consuming but extremely expensive and often a huge waste of *energy*.

LaRussell has a very spiritual approach to his work. The "energy" piece is important. I have observed more times than I'd like to admit that when an artist's energy is not right, they end up caught in lies, scandals, illegal activities, and being misled by people who never had their best interest at heart. You know, the kind of people who would set you up or accuse you of something that you did not do? That kind of drama is all too familiar among entertainers, and although entertainment, music in particular, can seem like all fun and games when you start to mingle with other aspiring characters, it is important to remember that the stakes are so high that many people forget who they were before they got into entertainment. These same people are willing to do anything they can to get "theirs" even if it was never "theirs" in the first place. (Please re-read the section on not being a jealous artist so you won't become this person.)

The other important thing that LaRussell points out in this quote is to do "good business." Which means several things. When you are striving to be a good person, you will do good business, meaning being transparent and honest about every aspect of what you do, say, and promise others. To do good business also implies that you are keenly aware of the value of your art and not foolishly giving it away for free just to get "exposure" or pulling stunts to gain "clout."

When LaRussell talks about doing good business, it is all the things that I just mentioned, but it is also about being a good human who wants to do business with other moral, honest, and fair people. It is important that you treat all of your colleagues with respect, and they do the same for you. However, it is always important that you don't confuse colleagues for "friends."

Now, I will say that this is and always has been a tricky

proposition. There is no other industry in the world where you will meet people as creative, charismatic, attractive, and seductive as in the entertainment industry. It is a place where there is a lot of partying, and people's ability to resist the euphoria is usually at an all-time low. It is easy to meet people and be seduced when defenses are down. But on the other hand, the stakes are too high not to be vigilant. Artists can make a million dollars with one handshake, one date, or one guest appearance. Don't you think that everyone wishes that could happen to them? You may be the lucky one. And if you are, you will meet people who will be jealous of you as you progress in your journey. People you don't even know are watching your every move. They will do everything in their power to get some of what you have. There is a classic song from 1983 by UK artist Annie Lennox called *Sweet Dreams Are Made of This*. The lyrics are absolutely prophetic regarding the world of entertainment.

> *Some of them want to use you*
> *Some of them want*
> *to get used by you*
> *Some of them want to abuse you*
> *Some of them want to be abused*
> *Sweet dreams are made of this*
> *Who am I to disagree*
> *I travel the world and the seven seas*
> *Everybody's looking for something*
>
> Annie Lennox

These words exemplify the true conundrum of show business. You just never know the intent of the people that you are dealing with in the entertainment space. Just one false move or dealing with people who are not good people, and you can find yourself knee-deep in litigation before you know it.

While talking about the law, this leads me to the discussion of artists who do things that they always regret. Everyone has heard of rock stars and rap stars who trash hotel rooms, total new sports cars, and worse. When artists make these kinds of self-destructive mistakes, attorney Leron Rogers says, "It can be an expensive mistake, but things happen, and you have to adjust and do what is best for your client at the instance. I am here to mitigate the damage."

And, I might add, these contracts that you sign do not spell out that your bad behavior breaches the contract, but I am telling you, it always does. This is especially true when it comes to endorsement deals. As we discussed, a brand should be the foundation of your company's belief systems, whether it is the Nike brand or yours. When a company chooses you to represent their brand, there is a tacit understanding that you share the same values that they do. Your raucous action, which you may consider an innocent "mistake," can tarnish what this company has worked for decades to create. That should be the same way you feel about your own brand. We have just seen how quickly it can be taken away from an artist, no matter how successful. Just think, Ye went from billionaire back to millionaire just by spewing what many considered hateful anti-Semitic rhetoric. Think twice before doing something that you and your bank account will regret.

When I sat down with Leron Rogers, I asked him to give me a comprehensive list of questions that an artist should ask an attorney when looking for representation. This is the list:

- How long have you been doing this?
- Who are some of the artists that you represent?
- What is your fee structure?
- Do you have time (bandwidth) to take on a new artist right now?
- Will someone else be handling my day-to-day business? And who will that be, and what is their experience?
- If I am in a tight situation, can you get to my issue right away?

He also generously gave me a list of questions that artists need to know before signing a contract:

- Besides the financial terms, what are the material terms?
- What is the number of albums expected in this contract?
- What are the royalty rates?
- What are 360 percentages, and how are they defined?

360 percentages is a term that is also referred to as *ancillary rights* or *passive participation*. The reason to ask your lawyer about it is that it is a tricky area that requires an entertainment lawyer's expertise. Your potential lawyer understands that record companies want nothing more than to participate in every aspect of your creativity, including streaming, touring, merchandise, acting, books, etc. However, a savvy lawyer knows that they are not entitled to your acting. For example, if you are playing a fictional character unrelated to your musical persona. If an artist has an established social media following and he/she chooses to engage their audience through social media, the record label is not entitled to that income either. It is a nuanced point that could save an artist a lot of money. It is definitely worth inquiring about.

- Is Net Profit Off Gross Income or Adjusted Gross?

This should always be defined in the contract. Gross profit is something that your lawyer has to negotiate down to an adjusted amount, such as 25-35 percent for deduction expenses which often include paying your agent, commissions, attorneys fees, etc. This is important because if not solidly defined in the contract, a record label may say they want "10 percent gross of your appearances." Your lawyer will make sure that their portion is from the *net* income and not the gross. The "net" takes into consideration an artist's other obligations, as mentioned above. This can be clearly defined in the contract and is always subject to negotiation.

- Are My Publishing Rights Included in the Agreement?

They shouldn't be, and a lawyer will make sure that your publishing rights are a separate deal.

HUNGRY BUT NOT THIRSTY

There's an undeniable hunger dream chasers have. This hunger must never turn into thirst. Thirsty people are the easiest to prey upon, and, make no mistake about it, in this business, people will prey on you if they sense that you are thirsty. When you start on this journey, you must do it with an openness and willingness to build brick-by-brick if you want to get to the finish line.

I've often experienced artists who feel cornered. They are in such a desperate situation at home; perhaps they have a child on the way or are sleeping on a friend's couch with nowhere else to go. This artist, reasonably so,

> *Be warned: Shortcuts almost always lead to exits. You need to be extremely careful when people offer you shortcuts in this business.*
>
> J.R. McKee

could be thirsty. And when a predatory crook senses this, they will come along and offer a "shortcut" deal. The person offering this deal knows it is not a good deal, but they know that at this moment, for the artist, the money is all that they will see.

If you find yourself in a desperate situation and you feel

that what you are being offered is not a great deal, do not take it. My candid advice is, pass on the deal and work even harder because you are close. The truth is, if you didn't already have what it takes, the deal would not have been offered to you in the first place. Think about it.

COMMANDMENT

8

IT TAKES A VILLAGE

*"If you want to go quickly, go alone.
If you want to go far, go together."*

African proverb

You Need Believers

Art is a commodity, and as the artist, you are your own business. Art businesses usually start with you, an individual artist with the talent and the vision. What most artists discover sooner than later is that running an artistic enterprise becomes too cumbersome to handle while also trying to stay inspired in order to create their art.

> You get the people who are best in their field. Now, it means you are not just getting it done. Instead, you are getting it done right.
>
> Eric Bellinger, Artist

Having a team in place increases the possibility for you to grow your business exponentially. With a solid infrastructure, your business will start to hum along, reaching wider audiences and increasing your income.

In the beginning, artists normally have to handle a lot of the day-to-day responsibilities. That's actually a good thing because it gives you an understanding of what it takes to get certain things done and how you like them done. The key is to be well-educated in all aspects of your business so it is easier to see it as an actual business. Again, study the courses I offer at sharedinformation.co

The great thing about the time you, as an artist, spend taking care of all the tasks (like answering emails, booking shows, paying the studio, etc.) is that you should gain a solid understanding of what it takes to handle your career properly. With that being said, your experience with the day-to-day tasks allows you to replace yourself with someone who can do the same job you did, but better because that will be their only focus. As the head of the operation, you will know exactly what they should be doing because you've done it. Although handling it all alone feels comfortable and safe, there will come a time when this will not be possible with the big dreams ahead.

So, let's say the time is now. I would advise you not to get stuck giving titles to your team members. One reason for this is that titles hold no weight if people aren't living up to them. The other thing to consider about titles, it pigeonholes individuals who may be needed to add support in other areas that their title doesn't address. It's just one less reason for anyone on the team to say, "That's not my job."

The proper way to build out a team is to start considering where you and your operations are weakest. What in your operation is lagging behind? Do you always forget to return calls? Do you not get to the post office often enough to ship your art? Have you engaged enough fans this week? Do you forget to pay bills because they aren't signed up for autopay?

You might also take a minute to think about the day-to-day non-creative tasks that leave you feeling uninspired. Do you hate booking appearances? Does it show because you don't have any coming up in the next few months? Where is your social media campaign lacking? Has it been two months since you posted any brand-relevant material?

It will behoove you to take a step back and seriously consider where you need the most help.

Once you do that, I suggest that instead of saying I need a manager, you can prioritize your list of tasks, naming the tasks you need to cover the most, and then you can start to build your team, one taskmaster at a time.

I recommend that you start building your team by looking at your inner circle of trusted friends, family, and acquaintances. In addition to finding people who are excellent at organization, for example, you are also looking for someone who is flexible and willing to do new things. But most importantly, when looking for all of your eventual team members, you must make sure the people that you choose are believers. When considering this person and even when interviewing them about the position, it is crucial that they share *your* vision for your career. Find believers with the skill sets that you lack and a work ethic that matches yours. That is how you build a team.

DREAM TEAM

Not to be redundant, but building a team is one thing; building a dream team is the difference between being an artist and being a superstar. When an artist is building his or her team, it is crucial that the artist really knows the people he/she is putting on their team, as well as knows some of the intangible things about this person. What is their past experience, and how well will it translate to being on your team? How are they with money? Are they trustworthy? Do they have good credibility? How do they handle their own lives (spouses, children, household)? Do they use drugs? Do they waste money on useless things? Do they often complain about not having enough money? Are they in excellent health? These questions seem outrageous to ask a prospective team member (possibly family or old friend), but as you enter into a business agreement that will tether you to this individual for a long time, these are actually very wise questions, and they will remove all of the avoidable scenarios that we hear about on social media a little too often.

Now, just to help you with imagining your dream team, I maintain everything that I have said, which means hiring your team one at a time as your needs grow. Just having one person on your team will make a huge difference immediately. Music industry guru Bryan Calhoun says, "Staffing up with 'your boys' can work if your best friend is a CPA with experience in the music industry. OK, you can work with him. Loyalty is important, but finding trustworthy people who can do the job correctly is more so."

Caution is needed when building a team. However, as you envision your business eventually thriving, I asked Leron Rogers to give me a sense of a really solid team for a musician, and this is what he said. (Again, do not take on too many people at once, but this is what it can look like when your songs are selling and streaming, and you are touring, and the infrastructure is in place).

Manager: Your manager will act as the co-CEO of you

and your art. They will act as your partner who will conduct all of your business pertaining to your music, content, and your contractual agreements and obligations. They will be your spokesperson behind the scenes, and they are your mouthpiece for your brand. They are your sole contact with the outside world. And, they make deals happen.

Digital Content Manager: This person manages all aspects of your social platforms: timing, content, and strategizing on how to boost fan engagement in ways that are in alignment with your brand. This person manages your online presence and should have photography and video skills to help create content.

Day-To-Day Assistant: An organized, smart, articulate person you trust with everything. This person will act on your behalf, take your phone calls, and make phone calls you don't want to make; this person knows what you like and don't like; they know your favorite foods; they know of your medical concerns and how to alleviate them and how to help you when your day is stressful. This person is a problem solver.

Tour Manager: A touring person must know the ins and outs of moving you and your team and band from one place to another seamlessly. They should be knowledgeable about routes using buses, trains, and airplanes. They should also be savvy about the costs to travel; clean, affordable accommodations; check-in and check-out times; what amenities are available in the areas of the hotels; etc. This person would also be responsible for paying drivers and hotel bills, making sure the artist and team are out on time, setting up early check-ins or late check-ins, etc. This person is also responsible for giving tickets and backstage access to the media and your invited guests.

Brand Manager: This person knows your brand keys and can recite them in their sleep. They should be able to articulate them and keep the whole team adhering to the principles set by the brand keys at all times. This person is also in charge of public relations. Handling requests for interviews, working with the touring person to make sure that key members of the press have access to shows and after-show interviews, etc. This person should be actively looking to pair you with other brands; they must be a deal seeker and maker.

Whew! That's a lot of people and a lot of responsibilities, and the list can continue to grow. You may notice that some of these responsibilities could possibly overlap, which is why all of your team members must be ready and willing to work together, a trait not everybody carries. Be careful because a bad team player can ruin the morale of your team. Again, this is a list of possible positions/titles, and the dream of having all of these filled at the start of your career is *ludicrous.* Do not rush to fulfill all of these roles as a beginning artist to feel like you are bigger than you are. I just thought it would be helpful to give a sense of what your career can and will look like if you follow the *10 Artist Commandments* and play all of your cards right!

TIME VS. MONEY

When it comes to business, a lot of our decisions are based around money when in fact, time is the most valuable asset, *not* money. It often happens that artists get stingy, not wanting to pay someone to do what they could do on their own. You saw the list of tasks necessary to make an artist's career flourish. If you are in charge of creating beautiful music and movies or writing amazing books, why do you think that you have the extra time to route the cities and book the venues for your own tour? If you hire the right person, not only will it be done seamlessly while you are shooting the music video for your song, you'd get two things done simultaneously that would not have happened if you had to do both. Inevitably, one of the two tasks would suffer. The tour would be delayed because the venues aren't booked, or your new album wouldn't have great music videos to promote it.

Don't be afraid to hire the right people to do tasks that you no longer have the time to do. And if it is a question of cash flow, you can always negotiate to pay a percentage of a given event or arrange to pay them later. Who would say no to being a part of something that is on its way to greatness? Remember, if this person can save you time so you can do what you do better, it is one hundred percent worth it. That is how businesses scale, by putting the right people in the right place so the artist has free time to look at the bigger picture and build bigger visions for themselves and the team.

SINK OR SWIM

When bringing on teammates, it is best to give them clear and precise directives on what their job will be. This is necessary because you need to be able to hold them accountable for their responsibilities. (See the list above to know what you should expect from your team members.) Once the directives are given, it's best not to micromanage them. You're bringing them in because they possess a certain skill set that you likely do not, which means stepping out of their way and allowing them to do what they do best and better than you.

The other important part about having a team around you is that you must be realistic and not be afraid of one or more team members not working out. Some people may need to be demoted or let go immediately, and some people may need to be promoted. But this will be impossible to decipher if you stick your nose in every detail and don't allow people to sink or swim. Just like everything else in business, assembling your team is also trial and error. Don't lock yourself into long-term contracts unless the two of you have already proven to work well together.

With every step up the ladder comes new obstacles. Some people may rise to the occasion while others struggle to grow with you. As the saying goes, "You can't take everyone to the top with you." When you begin to feel this stress with your team, it may be time to restructure. This doesn't automatically mean firing everyone or even one person. While, of course, that could be necessary. But it does mean that something or some people need to change. There needs to be a shift in responsibilities to relieve some of the pressure. Maybe new teammates need to be added, or certain teammates need fewer, more, or different responsibilities. There's no perfect structure for a team. The goal is to have a system that runs smoothly and everyone understands their responsibilities and can handle them.

CEO

The truth is that as an artist, you are the face of your business. So, if anything goes wrong, no matter whose fault it may have been, you will be blamed. The headlines won't say the manager's name, the assistant's name, or the bus driver's name; it will say YOUR NAME in large bold letters. With this being fact, you have no choice but to always be in full control of your business. Your career, no matter how many partners you have, is completely in your hands. If your business falls off, your team members will go to the next artist. You cannot make the mistake of placing your career in someone else's hands. Your partners are your trusted advisers, and I do advise you to listen to them and take what they tell you in full consideration, but you must always make the final decision. You are the CEO. It's just the cost of having your name in lights.

Instinct

I haven't spoken too much about instinct in this book because I believe that it's crucial to have a structured approach to turning your art into a business to ensure your freedom to make as much money as you desire. I will also say that I am a rebel in many respects. I make a lot of my decisions using my instincts and the talent that I have. When asked about how I structure my budgets with my artists, I had to admit I have never had a filter on this. I'll spend everything; I am not a budgeter. If I believe in the artists, they will work out. My wins have far exceeded my losses.

Despite my saying that, most people have to and should budget. So even I have to put the reins on, sometimes. The only reason I can say that about myself is that I have years of experience watching artists soar and drop. I have learned to understand why and how. More realistically speaking, I try to have only three artists, max, at one time.

Most labels are not built to be detail-oriented when it comes to the individual artists. For my successful artists, it never comes to the point that I've spent too much on one because the success erases the debt of capital I invested into them. There are certain characteristics and values that must exist in order to become successful. Normally it comes down to an artist's work ethic and confidence. Sometimes artists lack certain crucial skill sets. Just for the record, I have never dropped an artist because I've spent too much money on them. It mostly happens if I see that the artist is missing certain characteristics that have nothing to do with their talent. Sometimes it's a lack of confidence or, more often, a lack of work ethic. Sometimes their head just isn't in the right space yet. Not yet. Remember, sometimes a "no" just means "not yet."

9

BUSINESS IS BUSINESS

*"I'll keep it short and sweet. Family. Religion.
Friendship. These are the three demons that you
must slay if you wish to succeed in business."*

Matt Groening, Cartoonist

ARTREPRENEUR

The major mistake artists make is not being upfront about the uncomfortable truths about business. And because no one ever talks about it, the ugly truths perpetuate. There are millions of sayings and warnings about the harshness of business in general, but even more when it comes to the entertainment industry. One of these adages is that "There are friends in life, but there are no friends in business."

Especially in entertainment, where personality is the number one key to an artist's success, it is painfully easy to fall into "friendship" with most people in entertainment. Who doesn't want to befriend the hottest, most beautiful person in the room or the most connected? Unfortunately, you never know who is who, so we get involved too quickly and with people who are looking for something to help themselves.

> *Someone once told me Business first and Business second.*
>
> Eric Bellinger

Sadly, these warnings are most pertinent in big cities where music, writing, fine art, film, and television business are predominant. The unspoken truth is that everyone wants to get famous and/or everyone wants to get rich in these places. It's as simple as that. When you go to visit Burlington, Wisconsin, you NEVER meet a person who has left their family in another state or country to be in Burlington, Wisconsin, because they have come to get famous. That is not the case in cities like Los Angeles, New

York, or even Atlanta. Those cities are known as being particularly fast-paced, cutthroat, and super competitive. Those are the only three cities that I can safely say that everyone moves to for money, fame, and power.

Where there is art and glamour, there is also a lot of money. It's as simple as that. This conversation does not exclude your friends and your family. Often even your friends and family want to somehow make a living off of *your* art in any way they possibly can. That is why you hear of siblings selling their famous brother's story or incriminating photos to celebrity blogs all the time.

What makes the idea of business so uncomfortable is that it exposes a deep truth that exists in each one of us. It is that in business, you want to make money for yourself. And you want to make the most money possible. Business *is* the one place where you should be selfish because, for the most part, your tireless efforts should be rewarded by high visibility (fame) and monetary gain. Because the stakes are so high and it is possible that a lot of people can be hurt, a proper business needs structure and a solid financial infrastructure, and that is what I suggest you have when you decide to go for it.

If your friends are going to be a part of your

> *Someone told me you don't have any friends in this industry. You hear that a lot, but I have been in it; you realize that you have to know your price and add tax. People are going to do what benefits them. It is transactional.*
>
> BluJune, Songwriter

business, they need responsibilities and clear compensation for those responsibilities. Even if there's no money today, set in place what they will make when the money comes. This will save you a world of headaches down the road and likely save you from having a friend in your business that can't handle the responsibilities but perhaps said they could in anticipation of payday. Think of the thousands you will save by not having an incompetent person feeding off of your career and not holding up their end of the agreement.

Business is all about truth, and I am all about truth. So, the truth is that a successful artist's average career span is three years. Imagine working for years in the studio, weekends on the road, and hours in front of your phone creating content. Think of all those years you spent climbing the ladder to success to feed your family.

Let's just say after many years, you finally break through and get your first hit record. Your dream has come true, and everyone is talking about you. This is the moment you have been waiting for your whole life. Now imagine a hard truth: In less than three years after your moment, it may be over already. No one's checking for you, and your label isn't returning your calls. You may manage to get a few more shows for a quarter of what you're used to being paid. By year five, you're back home where it all started, broker than you were before the dream came true.

For the majority of artists whose careers look like that, it is because of their lack of understanding of the intricate nuances and unspoken elements of the entertainment business. Having a hit record puts an incredible spotlight on an artist. The hype that a popular song can create can make you a star almost overnight. Eventually, when the hype of your song wears down, you probably haven't considered how to operate your art as a business, which is what it was all along, but only you didn't get it. Sadly, artists with this conundrum have a team behind them that were equally unprepared because they were not carefully selected. A team like that has no loyalty and is there only to get what it can; when the ship begins to sink, they'll jump to the next artist who will just as foolishly hire them.

Although *10 Artist Commandments* isn't a financial book, financial malpractice is the number one problem in this hit-record-hangover scenario; it happens to the majority of artists that burn through all the cash they've received, or worse, it gets burned through for them because they didn't properly set up their business.

This is what I refer to when I speak of the structure that a business needs. As I mentioned in Commandment #7: Lawyer Up, your first priority when building your team should be a lawyer. Having the right lawyer in place from day one can protect you from this unfortunate scenario altogether. A lawyer will have advice and guidance about the people you bring onto your team. A lawyer will assist in making contractual agreements with these team members that will protect you and your interests. Your lawyer will also ensure that your original contracts protect you from bad deals, which guarantees that you are not leaving money on the table or that your money is not going to someone undeservingly. Another thing that having a lawyer will protect you from is not giving inappropriate responsibilities to your team members (entourage). You could find yourself justifying missing funds or excessive, unauthorized expenditures based on trusting people's words because of your history with them; I guarantee you will have leeches burning through your cash, all in the spirit of being "homies." The blind trust of an old friend dissipates quickly when there is money involved, which is where the importance of financial infrastructure comes into play.

Whatever agreement you reach with your team members should be in writing so there is no need to worry about blurred lines with the distribution of funds.

Another cardinal sin I've seen committed by non-business-minded artists is not having cash reserves for investing back into your business or for emergencies. In the fast pace of entertainment, emergencies are always lurking around the corner. Imagine being on the road, and your bus breaks down, and you have to be at your show in eight hours. It will take two days to fix the bus. A good business person will have reserves. Perhaps you need to get another bus or hire a different driver or fly to the venue so you don't miss the show. This is not a time to be looking around at your team because they will all say they are broke. It will be on you and the senior members of your team to get to the show at all costs. At that moment, money should never be the showstopper since you have been making money all along and should be prepared.

Despite the dismal statistics that the average artist's career lasts for only three years, there is good news that should make you feel better. There are artists whose careers can last ten years or more. Think of Drake or Rick Ross. Do you know why? Because those artists have taken their careers into their own hands. Besides being recording artists, they have become entrepreneurs, and Drake has become one of hip-hop's best A&Rs, consistently collaborating with new talent and helping them rise to fame. Trust me, the benefit of that isn't one-sided. Rick Ross is a serial entrepreneur owning multiple food chains and real estate, which in turn ensures he always has money to invest in his latest album and never has to depend on a label. In order to grow and/or sustain any business, you must reinvest in it. And make no mistake about it, no matter who your partner or label is, it is inevitable that one day there will be a creative, financial, or legal disagreement that can change your relationship irreversibly. A record label's business structure is airtight and is ready to take on whatever challenge may come its way. What preparation looks like is having cash and having a structure in place. Trust me; the challenges will come, so don't make the mistake of not preparing for down while you're up.

A Lifetime Student of the Game

As the CEO of your business, it's in your absolute best interest to stay aware of every change and twist in the industry. With numerous new technologies emerging every single day, not only is user interface changing drastically, but so is the nature of deal structures, streaming, royalties, and privacy issues. Being well-educated on these entities should start the day you decide you want to seriously pursue your art career as an "artrepreneur." With the proper knowledge of how the business works, you can conceive a plan to succeed in that business. To be the best at your art may be the ultimate goal, but there are many great artists out there that we'll never hear from because they couldn't navigate the game. Don't let that be your excuse.

10 Artist Commandments is your first step to educating yourself on seeing your creative talent as a sustainable business for years to come. When you succeed at reaching your goals, don't make the fatal mistake of turning a blind eye to your business. Continue to keep your hands and eyes on the business and forever stay a student of the game. That's how you'll win.

> *By failing to plan, you are preparing to fail.*
>
> Benjamin Franklin

COMMANDMENT

10

ADAPT OR DIE

"Adaptability is not imitation. It means the power of resistance and assimilation."

Mahatma Gandhi

NATURAL LAW

The law of nature is to adapt or die, and human beings have survived for centuries because of our natural instinct to adapt. As your environments change, you need to be willing to shift with them in order to survive. You will need to change your survival tactics as you enter a new setting. The natural law must also be applied to your art as an artist. If you were used to connecting with fans in person before Covid, I am sure you had to adapt to the new mandates where meet and greets, concerts, art galleries, festivals, museums, and spoken-word events were completely shut down. I already applaud you without knowing what you did, but if you were still sharing your art throughout the pandemic, I know you had to think outside of every box there ever was.

I have witnessed something so amazing over the past decade. I've seen artists adapt when the world shifted from physical media to digital media and record stores converted to Apple Music, 106 & Park to YouTube, and when artists with two million friends on Facebook and 500 thousand followers on Instagram had to take their talents to TikTok and dance, edit, and recreate their message to include viral trends on that new platform. Without being too presumptuous, just knowing the nature of things, it is clear to me that as artists, if we don't adapt to change, our careers will die. We have all worked too hard for that to happen.

THINGS WILL CHANGE

Change is inevitable and can be scary. Humans are creatures of habit. We intuitively memorize the aisles of our favorite supermarket so we can get in and out faster because we know where everything is. You get gas at the same gas station because you know the cashier; you know that on Sunday night, dinner is at six at your mother's house. When any of those things change just a little, it can make you feel everything from unsteady to angry. Why did they change your supermarket to a Whole Foods? Why is the gas station now going to be high-rise condos? Why did your mother get married and no longer makes Sunday dinner for you? Why do changes happen when what was happening before was working just fine?

Once you get over the change and explore the new, you may enjoy the changes in your routine. The new Whole Foods may have better produce; the new high-rise condo may make the neighborhood look better. And your mother's new husband may be taking her out on Sundays, which makes her happier than she's ever been, which is amazing for you both because when your mom smiles, you can't help but smile.

If you can find it in your heart to look at change as a positive, your career is already one step ahead because you are open to being flexible, which is really the name of the entertainment game across all mediums.

Usually, change is choosing new methods to advance with the current culture. When one thing changes, it always has to do with something else. The new Whole Foods in your neighborhood is directly related to the new high-rise condos. The demolition of the gas station may be because the analytics for the condo showed that more people in the neighborhood would drive electric cars or use bicycles to commute. (That is analytics at its best.)

But seriously, think about how advanced technology has changed entertainment in ways that we could have never imagined. It has changed the autonomy, creativity, and capacity to connect directly to the audience in ways that make entertainment an industry that is more accessible to any and everyone.

Can you imagine still having to sit at a computer and download each of your favorite songs to an MP3 player or iPod? How inconvenient would it be to have to carry a box cell phone around versus sliding your device in and out of your pants pocket or purse? How much time would be taken away from your creativity if you had to draw the same design over and over rather than being able to print the same design on multiple articles of clothing using a silk screen printer? Look around you at all of the hundreds of thousands of people with AirPods in their ears because they were tired of rolling up and having long cords in the way when simply listening to music, watching videos or movies, and making phone calls. New innovations are designed to make life easier. And you, as an artist, can use them to make your art and life better and more productive. And with more productivity is more money and success. Don't ever be afraid of change. Embrace it.

The wisest people understand that with new technologies come new opportunities. The reward for being an early adapter always outweighs the risk of being unfamiliar with something new. Every day there are new ways to reach your audience, new ways to tell your story, and likely new ways to create multiple revenue streams. A lot of brands get stale over time (decades), and new platforms usually open new doors for those companies, giving them new life. Never stop being open to new technologies because, as things shift, you don't want to be left behind. Because when the convenience of new technologies takes hold of the psyche of the masses, what you're used to doing will become obsolete.

If you were to start selling CDs out of the trunk of your car as the only form of marketing and promoting your new music, you probably would not become successful, whereas fifteen or twenty years ago, that is literally how independent artists marketed their art. Now, if you are making music, you can upload music to a digital streaming site and reach fans all over the world and sell signed CDs at your shows as something personal for your fans to have forever. This is the same for writers: If you sold self-published books in front of Barnes & Noble, I doubt you would obtain the same success as if you sold your books online. The journey from artist to consumer has come a long way. Having a middleman used to be the best way for an artist to get their art to the public. Now, artists have adapted to media changes and are now able to reach millions of people with a click of one button from the comfort of their own homes. Not to mention the amazing leaps and bounds technology has taken. Musicians can literally record an album on their phones. Artists, this is our time. Never be afraid to learn and try new things. I promise it will improve your bottom line.

I started my record label when I was twenty-one years old. At the time, Myspace was the dominant digital platform, and in 2006, I built my first artist, Tha Joker, into one of the biggest rap artists on that platform. This digital streaming success helped launch my whole career. By the time I signed my second artist, K Camp, I thought I was a pro and had no intentions of changing anything about what I was doing.

But as they will, things shifted, and Myspace was no longer the dominant platform. To my surprise, the natural law presented itself, and I needed to find a completely different way to break K Camp. I took what I already knew and went back to the drawing board and discovered new ways to expand and adapt to the changes happening in the music industry. It was not easy, but I adapted until I got it right.

Not to rain on your current technological parade, but I have to break it to you that what works today will not work forever. However, if you build a tight enough foundation around your artistry, you won't have to completely restructure every single time something changes. This is called preparation. Allow your talents to live on forever by not placing yourself in a box and stay willing to adapt without straying too far from your initial intentions. But also understand that all artists have to be prepared to shift in any season to maintain relevance. Songwriter Blu June is in the middle of her star rising but is already planning her next moves. "In order to adapt, I had to figure it out. I asked myself, how can I get to that space and still be myself? How do I deliver my songs that resonate? We learned to adapt. I realized that I can write pop songs but do it with an R&B style. "I have a songwriter friend who says, 'I will never cross over and do pop.' He doesn't have any placements either."

Take Beyoncé for another example; she rarely gives interviews, and when she does, she doesn't usually address her family, marriage, rumors, or emotions too much; but she knows that she needs to stay connected to her fans and addresses these topics more in-depth with her self-produced documentaries and visuals that meet the needs of her fans but on her terms. Mrs. Carter has such a tightly-oiled machine around her that she didn't lose one bit of visibility because she chose not to interview. Instead, she figured out ways to keep up the standard need for information into her private life but made the industry adjust to her and the way she would get that information out.

Remember Beyoncé's surprise album drop with no promo, marketing, or press, launching in the middle of the night? No one had ever dropped an album that way before. This release stunned everyone, and the shock alone at this unheard-of method of dropping a new release became its own promotional tool. Now, we see more artists dropping music at random as well. Beyoncé is a pioneer; she recognized the new times and technologies and took full advantage of them.

The normal way for celebrities to keep themselves relevant in the past was to go on press tours that included radio, television, magazine, and red-carpet interviews. However, as the industry and technology advance, opportunities arise; artists are able to promote themselves online via their personal accounts and avoid the platforms they don't like. Sometimes, YOU can be the change you want to see and move the needle for everyone else. Remember we talked about that "next-level" artist? Could it be you? You just have to be bold enough to do something so outrageous that you alone can change the game. Again.

CROWD SURFING

Social media platforms, apps, and media outlets will constantly come and go. I had to learn that the hard way with Myspace. However, the need for an artist to have an engaged audience and fan base will never change. Platforms will shift, but crowds and fans will always have the same hunger for talent that moves them.

It is now the artist's job to find their audience because no two platforms are the same. Twitter (now, X) does not work like Instagram, and TikTok does not work like Facebook (Meta). Each outlet requires getting around the learning curves. You must educate yourself on how media platforms work and create the necessary content to earn success in growing your community. If you're paying attention, it will be fairly easy to spot what platforms attract which crowd. On the flip side, it is a little harder figuring out how to stay on brand with each platform when they are all so different. The answer is to use your analytics to find out which content is attracting the most engagement on that particular platform and decide how you can create more of that content without straying away from your initial brand keys. You can stay on top if you consistently meet your audience where they are by presenting your brand in fresh, new, and exciting ways.

If your audience is used to seeing you post behind-the-scenes (BTS) clips from music videos or painting or writing sessions, and they love it, don't stop posting BTS footage. But if this type of content starts to bore you, you can always find new ways to incorporate BTS footage. Perhaps, you can start including your team if you don't already. Instead of just showing yourself doing your thing in front of the camera, let your audience see what it looks like when your engineer is mixing and mastering your newest songs, how your cameraman sets up his cameras and lighting, how you prepare before painting a portrait, how you outline a manuscript before writing, or how you feel out a beat before writing a song. Creating comes more naturally when the content comes from your everyday life. Don't think too hard about what to produce. Think about why your audience follows you and use that to your advantage when coming up with new ideas. All I ask is that you stay on brand. What are your three brand keys again?

_____ _____ _____

Have they changed during the course of reading this book? If they have, that's good. It means you are really working on it.

TRANSLATE YOUR STORY

Although you will always be telling your story, the key is finding new mediums to reach a broader audience as you attract diversity. Reaching new audiences isn't difficult since platforms are steadily emerging, and there are constantly new ways to tell the same story. The way you tell your story on Twitter (now, X) with 280 characters per tweet is totally different from the way you can tell your story on TikTok, using crazy editing effects with a sixty-second video. If your mission is to spread your story as far and wide as possible, take advantage of every avenue available for marketing because you never know which avenue will be the one that leads you straight to the top. Songwriter Blu June and her partner, Chi, of Nova Wav, are adapting by taking their production skills and using them for DJing. Think of the whole new audience they will reach.

Author Miguel Ruiz said, "God, the supreme artist, uses our life for the creation of art. We are the instruments through which the force of life expresses itself." Adaptation means growth and expansion. It does not mean turning your back on what was; it is a call to innovate to make it greater. I, too, have nostalgia for what was: cassette tapes, vinyl, and VCRs. Actually, it is still great to cherish physical media in a digital world because we all can benefit from the character that older mediums lend to the newer (sometimes) too-perfect sound. Think of all of the artists who sample the skipping sounds of analog recordings and vinyl.

However, ingenuity is the birth of all great things. And as an artist, you have the special anointing to tell stories about what is and what can be. Artistry must always keep the future in sight. As artists, I ask you to embark on the journey of your craft with freedom and insight.

I leave the future in your delicate hands. Innovate and create new sounds, and delve into areas you have never gone before. Your courage shows the world what is possible. Use your art for *good*.

In *10 Artist Commandments,* I hope that I have given you new ways to succeed with your art financially, connectively, and creatively. Engage your fans, shower them with the truth of who you are, and show them who they can be. Do not emulate; create as only *you* can. Always do your best, and believe in your art. It's original. Collaborate with others, do not compete, and you will see the power of connecting.

As the artistic community grapples with the slippery

slope called AI, some of us worry about our livelihoods. We shouldn't. God made you to show the world who we are and should be. Remember, God makes no mistakes. Artists, please use your art to save this complex world. Never settle for a computer generating what only you can. Computers will never have the heart to tell the truth of our world. Artists hold the truth.

CONCLUSION

After eighteen years in the entertainment industry, I have been blessed to witness the alchemy that occurs when talented individuals with raw talent and a dream get to work. I stumbled into this business with my eyes set on simply being an entrepreneur. Music was not my first choice. But the very first time I saw producer Big Fruit in the studio, I called my father and said, "Dad, I'm literally watching magic."

After our first hit single, when we toured the US and made the label millions, we came home empty-handed. It was then that I learned that this magic is also a lucrative product, and if seen through entrepreneurial eyes, it could save lives and create wealth for people who never thought wealth was possible. I have been beyond blessed to meet incredibly talented creative people who write, sing, draw, and make movies and TV shows. They all understand work, money, vision, success, and, most importantly, they understand *freedom*.

As you know, entrepreneurism is at the center of my brand. And while constantly promoting the idea of self-reliance, I feel that I am doing important work for artists who deserve it. The sheer joy of making music with them is just the cherry on top.

It is my hope that *10 Artist Commandments* has been educational, enlightening, and inspiring to get you to see your gift in a whole new light. Your craft can feed you and your children for a lifetime if you embrace these ten pearls of wisdom presented in this book.

One of the most beautiful things that I see happening is that more and more artists are reaching back to put other artists on. They finally understand that there is always enough for everyone. The old days of being stingy with your limelight are quickly fading while collaboration has caught fire.

In closing, I will say that the best way for an artist to keep their spot at the top is to put other artists on. Too many times, as new generations rose, the older generation resented them instead of embracing them. Attaching yourself to or cosigning new acts only strengthens your position as an established artist. I love the example of George Clinton befriending the West Coast artists that gave his P-Funk a whole new life in the form of G-Funk. This resurgence added nearly two decades to George Clinton's relevance and a whole new appreciation of his groundbreaking legacy.

If you need further proof of this, look no further than the one and only Drake. Year after year, the 6 God picks some of the hottest, up-and-coming acts and jumps on their songs. A Drake feature is usually a career-launching opportunity for young artists. And guess what else? Being featured on emerging artists' records does no harm to Drake or his catalog. In fact, it usually just adds another hit to his successes. It keeps Drake visible and paid without the pressure of dropping his own new hit.

What I love about the entertainment industry is that there is enough for everyone. Up until now, that fact has been a best-kept secret. Only when artists can see their own magnificence and are ready to make it their life's work will they benefit from the message of *10 Artists Commandments*. Artists are chosen people. Their art is their legacy. Helping them realize that it's a business is what I'm here for.

—*J.R. McKee*

ACKNOWLEDGMENTS

This book is a culmination of my eighteen years in the music industry. It's all of my successes and failures while navigating how to create wealth as an entrepreneur in music. This career began thanks to my Grandma Ava suggesting and allowing me to throw college parties at her nightclub "421" in Starkville, Mississippi. It was there that I met DJ Redman, who introduced me to a local artist J-Money, who in turn introduced me to Cadillac Don and my eventual business partner Leland "Big Fruit" Clopton. Those guys took me under their wing and set me on this eighteen-year journey, so it's them whom I must first acknowledge. Secondly, I must acknowledge my father, who raised me to be an entrepreneur. Without this training, I am sure my stint on the road with Cadillac Don & J-Money would have been just a moment of fun instead of an eye-opening opportunity to create wealth. I must acknowledge the artists who have personally put their careers in my hands. I want to thank Tha Joker, Nation, Terrific, K Camp, Marissa, Blu June, Jacob Latimore, Garren, Feyi, Damar Jackson, Q Money, Muni Long, Amari Noelle, and Mannywellz. As well as the artists I've been able to guide along the way: Thank you, Rod Wave, Lil Durk, H.E.R., DJ Chose, YFN Lucci, LaRussell, Justine Skye, French Montana, and all the others whom I've contributed to because your wins and losses contributed to the heart of these 10 Commandments. I want to thank my editor, Kim Green, for turning the *10 Artist Commandments* into the life-changing book you are currently holding. I'd also like to thank my longtime friend since high school, Derick McMullin, for beautifully designing this book and the logos that coincide with it. Lastly, I must thank God not only for the vision to write this book but for what this book will go on to become.

About
the Author

J.R. McKee's family was raised in the projects. What was instilled in the whole family was the value of getting a solid education. Many took heed, several becoming nurses and all of them becoming successful enough to leave the projects behind. Although J.R.'s father strongly believed that education is good, he also knew that entrepreneurism is *better*.

As a kid, J.R. spent his days reading and studying books written by self-made millionaires. To ensure he understood them, his Army Major father quizzed him on the content. And because he was trained to be consistent, he is still reading those books to this day. As a revered entertainment mogul, J.R. McKee's unusual generosity, focus, and dedication to artists and their craft has given him the Midas Touch.

The sky is the limit seems to be what entrepreneurism has meant to him. J.R. McKee's demonstrated self-determination and dedication to artists and their craft has given him the freedom to create an entertainment legacy that includes educating other artists to see their own worth and reap the benefits.

After 18 years of navigating and changing the entertainment landscape, J.R. McKee's ingenuity and gut instincts have made him responsible for creating some of the most notable independent R&B and hip-hop artists of this generation. Over the years, his passion for artistry and raw talent landed him in various multi-faceted positions. With each, he learned the ropes and envisioned the future. Having been a manager, producer and songwriter, his hero's journey has been extraordinary.

At just 20 years old, he partnered with producer/songwriter Leland "Big Fruit" Clopton, to start Family Ties Entertainment. Their first signing, Tha Joker enjoyed unexpected success because McKee promoted him on early streaming model, Myspace, and then dared to make it possible for Tha Joker's mixtapes to be available on iTunes. The label's next signing, K Camp, amazed the industry as his career skyrocketed from local hitmaker to a multi-platinum artist. Although Family Ties is no longer actively seeking new talent, he says, "It still exists in the sense that it holds a catalog that is worth millions of dollars."

These early victories were just the beginning of McKee's demonstrated gift for innovation. After many years of consulting artists and labels alike, he went on to propel small artists into much bigger arenas, like the top of the Billboard charts. As a manager, he introduced songwriter,

Blu June to Rihanna to co-write a platinum song that appeared on Rihanna's Grammy Award winning album, *Unapologetic.* He humbly says, "A lot of major artists come to me for consultation and I've helped them do extremely well." He remembers one artist who had gotten no traction on TikTok and after consulting with McKee, the artist went from no followers to 1 million in 60 days.

The accolades for J.R. McKee are endless, but his proudest achievements come from elevating artists mentally, financially and creatively. With his Shared Information, he says, "I knew that I wanted to teach, young entrepreneurs..." He quickly corrects himself. "Not teach, but *create* young entrepreneurs." A serial entrepreneur himself, J.R. McKee wants to create businesses that not only help artists have a new vision of their art but also turn the universal notion of the "starving artist" on its head.

He has been called, "a mindset changer," which he seamlessly claims. He says, "That's sort of my role in the world – to change people's mindsets." With that, he created an entire platform dedicated to teaching others all that he has learned. The business is appropriately named, Shared Information. Not only does he feature online entertainment seminars, he has created a video Master Class which walks aspiring artists/entrepreneurs through eight informative hours filled with priceless information about building an artistic career by utilizing the digital tools that can transform an artist's journey.

In addition to those educational opportunities under

the Shared Information umbrella, McKee has penned his first book, *10 Artist Commandments,* which details the ten most important things that artists need to know to build a sustainable and lasting career. He says of his impetus to write the book, "I've been a part of breaking probably 10 artists. There are industry executives who have never actually broken one. I know that the difference between me and them, is these 10 principles which are not common knowledge. People don't analyze like I did in the book. I feel like this could be the starting point for them to analyze their steps. You really have to have a roadmap and this book will give them leverage."

JR McKee's next enterprise, MPR Global, is a Distribution Company "with a soul." MPR is an acronym for the three things that illustrate the pillars of his empire: *Music, Power and Respect.* In alignment with his life's mission to teach artists their own worth, his Distribution company/record label offers artist-friendly terms, because he built a career working with artists and saw their struggles. Although MPR serves artists in the traditional ways, there is something very distinctive about MPR, which stems from McKee's acute understanding of what music was and what it has become. "When we started in 2021, our main focus was *content not* music. The distinction may seem slight, but it is significant. McKee explains, "We're more in the media business now than we are in the streaming business. We release one song a month, but we put out five pieces of content a day. And so, we're making more media than we are music. I started MPR with a focus on content creation. So, instead of hiring an A&R staff, I hired a staff of content creators. When we're looking for artists, we're looking for artists who are content creators *first*. So, the artists that we're signing are going to have a combination of both skills; they're going to be great content creators, and great music makers."

His thinking is revolutionary. "Artists who are content creators, have already created themselves. They have to have done that before I even take an interest. At the end of the day, MPR "amplifies" what already deserves attention. MPR focuses on R&B artists although there are exceptions such as LaRussell who is a rapper, but also a formidable social media presence, and a business owner with his own socially-focused mission. Proudly, McKee boasts, "MPR Global got our first Grammy with Muni Long whose *Hrs & Hrs* won for best R&B performance."

A visionary, a chameleon and an early adapter is what JR McKee is and will always be. It was not too long ago that he was known as the first and foremost streaming executive. No longer touting his streaming acumen, McKee, says, "I stopped using the hashtag streaming executive because it won't be relevant very much longer." I coined that term and now every label has a streaming executive. But funny enough, we're already leaving streaming." He predicts, "Pretty soon, all of the artists will be selling directly to the consumer, basically through the blockchain. So, what's going to happen is that artists can bypass the middleman. Most people want to support the artists themselves, right?"

A staunch advocate for artists being in charge of their

own destiny, his mission goes beyond economics. "If we want to change anything, as a people, we're going to need financial resources. We are very good at music, and we're very good at the arts. But we aren't very good at extracting the wealth out of it. It's been extracted from us because historically, we were not thinking like entrepreneurs. My mission is to get people to open their eyes and see that. I have to explain to them that as soon as you become an artist, you become an entrepreneur. It's just shifting their mindset.

J.R. McKee is a man of surprises. He says, "I feel like my 18 years of work in the music industry may be coming to a close. My book and my classes and everything that Shared Information has done was to inform and uplift." After much soul-searching, the young mogul has decided to use all that he has learned to delve deeper into other areas of entrepreneurism. Media, Tech, Real Estate and the development of family-friendly health products are all areas that are of interest to him. But his most surprising journey will be a return to his original passion: acting.

Most don't know that J.R. McKee graduated from the Cleveland School of the Arts in Cleveland, Ohio. He says, "I've always been very much into acting. I'm actually looking for an acting coach. I'm going to start preparing because I'm going to be doing TV and film producing our own shows. I want to play in some of them. So, the next couple of years, I'm just going to be preparing for that and writing scripts and developing my craft." The perfectionist adds, "You know, you don't want to go into anything untrained."

McKee says his devout faith is part of his decision to explore other avenues. With the shifting sands of the music industry, he says his wife and mother are particularly happy that he is slowly moving away from the urban music scene. He says, "People may be surprised that I am a man of faith, but I don't mind revealing it. You know, I gotta give God his glory wherever I can."

www.ingramcontent.com/pod-product-compliance
Lightning Source LLC
Chambersburg PA
CBHW031812190326
41518CB00006B/296